Stan Moog

FIRST EDITION

Library of Congress Cataloging-in-Publication Data

Mooneyham, W. Stanley (Walter Stanley).
    Dancing on the strait and narrow.

    1. Christian life—1960. I. Title.
BV4501.2.M575 1989   248.4   88-45991
ISBN 0-06-065922-X

89 90 91 92 93 HC 10 9 8 7 6 5 4 3 2 1

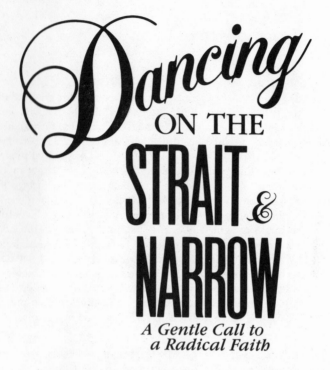

Dancing
ON THE
STRAIT &
NARROW

*A Gentle Call to
a Radical Faith*

Stan Mooneyham

1817

Harper & Row, Publishing, San Francisco

New York, Grand Rapids, Philadelphia, St. Louis
London, Singapore, Sydney, Tokyo

For Nancy,
my dance partner for life,
who helped me hear the music
and resonate to the beat

Contents

Preface vii

Introduction xv

1. Call to the Radical Life 1
2. How Strait? How Narrow? 12
3. Loving Beyond the Boundaries 24
4. Outrageous Forgiveness 36
5. Getting Even Is a High-Ticket Item 49
6. Matching the Inside and the Outside 59
7. The Myth of Being Perfect 73
8. What to Do with the Other You 85
9. Making Peace with Your Shadow 96
10. The Treasures of the Kingdom 107

Notes 119

Preface

I don't know exactly when I became aware that the old wineskin was splitting. I am sure the ferment had been going on unnoticed for several years. It started out quietly enough but became increasingly roisterous, until one day cracks appeared in the external covering and I became conscious of the heady smell of new wine.

By that time there was no stopping the fermentation process, even if I had wanted to. What was happening was intoxicating, disorienting, and outside my control.

It was also threatening—especially to one like myself, brought up in a rigid religious environment. Mine was a culture in which the boundaries of belief and behavior were defined by custom, community standards, and certain local authority figures. I took at face value the assurance that these rules governing faith and conduct were based in Scripture, but I now recall that slogans like "The Bible says it, I believe it, that settles it" took the place of questing, of inquiry, of discovery.

Even then such sloganeering seemed pretty shallow to me, especially since the "it" the Bible was supposed to settle was never defined. Everything people in authority wanted to have the final say about seemed to be covered. You could count on certain obvious and glaring transgressions of the flesh heading the list. You could also count on the more subtle sins of the spirit being ignored.

As I reflect on when the ferment within me started, I think I always resented having my thinking done for me. I wanted to reach conclusions on my own, free to stand apart from the common wisdom of my culture if that's where my understanding brought me.

However, when the collective goal is conformity and preservation of the intellectual status quo, you must learn quickly what is and what is not allowed. There are no written laws to guide you, no formal instruction to teach you. You simply learn. And you learn fast, and you learn well, because nothing will shape you up quicker than peer disapproval.

The fact that this system was not codified should not be construed as meaning that it was flexible. It wasn't. In my environment, open-mindedness was the eighth deadly sin. I wasn't sure if it necessarily qualified as a virtue, but I didn't think it deserved to be ranked up there with pride, sloth, and covetousness.

But in the absence of known alternatives, I bought into this system. If I may be allowed my youthful rebellions (routine stuff, nothing spectacular like Luther's Ninety-five Theses), my loyalty to that religious and cultural system served as a fairly decent way of controlling my urges toward becoming a completely self-directed missile. It met my need at the time for a surrounding structure to support my growth.

Nonetheless, in retrospect, I identify with Fynn (he uses only his first name) in his marvelous little book *Mister God, This Is Anna*.

Anna was a waif in London, a child of the streets with amazing insight. She could intuit more truth from observing than most people can learn in a classroom. Anna more or less adopted Fynn as a surrogate older brother, and in the book he shares what he learned at the feet of this child-teacher.

Of one of his encounters with her, he writes, "I shudder to think that . . . I was content to eat the stale bread of learning, when right under my nose Anna was busy baking new and crusty ideas."

Then continuing his culinary metaphor, Fynn says, "To me loaf and bread were synonymous. . . . In some part of my mind I can still detect a feeling of shame, a flicker of anger, and a sense of wasted time, from that moment when I realized that the important word was *bread*—that bread could be baked into an infinity of shapes. . . . The shape was nothing but a convenience. But my education had been too much concerned with the shapes. At odd moments I find myself angered when I ask the question, 'How much of what I was taught was a matter of convenience?'"[1]

Flynn's question is also mine, and much of the past few years of my life has been spent searching for an answer. I am no longer angry, but I do have a sense of wasted time. I owe a great debt to the religious systems of which I am a product, but I am also suspicious of them because they are still preoccupied with the shape of the loaf rather than the quality of the bread. How little of their concern has to do with truth, I wonder, and how much is merely a matter of convenience? I have enough empirical evidence of the latter to keep my skepticism robust and healthy.

The old wine started to taste flat as I developed a taste for the new. The fermentation process was inexorably under way.

I was feeling increasing discomfort in a lockstep environment, yet I didn't feel at home anywhere else. These were my people. I affirmed their basic beliefs. I still do, for that matter. After this manuscript was completed, I was talking about it with Dr. Carl F. H. Henry, my mentor for more than twenty years, and more important, my friend. He asked me an important question: "Where do you stand today on the historic creeds?"

My answer then and now is, "Flat-footed!" I had no problem during my growing-up years, nor do I now, in affirming as my own, without mental reservation, the beliefs set forth in the great creeds of the Church. Even then, I simply wanted the system to allow me the freedom to arrive at that position on my own, and I didn't understand why that wasn't permitted.

Today I am more sympathetic. I understand that mavericks are too disruptive and too threatening to a well-ordered system to be tolerated, much less endorsed. Yet I think the system loses a great deal in the long run by forcing out or freezing out the independent inquirers. Renewal and reform are impossible when all are required to think the same thoughts.

One must admit, however, that insistence on conformity is an effective means of self-preservation. But then, so is mummification.

It was not only the religious system that I found stifling. Everyone who is a public person, as I was before I abdicated the role, must sometimes feel that the pressures imposed by his or her constituency are more demanding than those laid on by peers. One feels "owned" by the multitudes, and someone seems always ready to assert a claim. I know that I found it extraordinarily difficult to be my own person; I was too busy trying to be what everyone else wanted me to be.

Colleagues had an idea of who they thought I should be as their leader. Weakness and doubt were not on their list of desirable qualities. Board members, who felt their own images to some degree tied up with mine, would have preferred a "safe" person as their representative. A maverick might do unconventional things that would reflect unfavorably on them. In my case, that was not only a possibility, it was a fact. I did embarrass them.

Donors to our organization frequently advised me about the kind of car I should drive, the neighborhood I ought to live in, how I should dress, and how much I should be paid.

Adding to the confusion created by this cacophony of voices were the conflicting views within these various publics. Few people seemed to have any regard or respect for my personal, real identity. Everyone wanted a role player, an after-dinner speaker who could get the big offering, a convention preacher who told the right stories to elicit maximum sacrifice and commitment. Because I believed the image had to be maintained, I accumulated a wardrobe of masks to be changed with each role I assumed.

Have I portrayed myself as an unwilling victim of this system? I'm afraid so, and that is not the whole truth. The fact is, I liked the payoff. For me, the payoff was applause and a growing reputation. What was pleasant to my ear was eminently satisfying to my ego.

But after a while I began to feel phony (which, in fact, I was) because I was not being true to myself. I became more a trademark for a cause than an individual person. When I ended my career as president of World Vision International after nearly fourteen years, I had begun to feel like the Betty Crocker of world hunger! The experience was, I can tell you, pretty vacuous.

Yet I often wished I could cork the ferment I felt inside or at least control it in some rational, orderly way. Having worked in the system for more than a third of a century, I knew the high stakes involved. For me, it was nothing less than my future security.

I am told that many prisoners who are released after long incarceration are terrified to face the uncertainty of life without the structure of the prison system and the security of a cell. I think my experience was not dissimilar.

It was during this scary time that I became aware that the old wineskin was splitting. I knew I could no longer ignore what was taking place. The longing for freedom, the need to strip off the masks, the desire to affirm my own identity were greater than the fear of disapproval, of loss of security, of abandonment of a cocoon, now empty.

The leaky old wineskin would serve its purpose no longer. Many of my friends shook their heads in perplexity and sadness as a white-haired man of fifty-seven summers joined his spiritual ancestor, Abraham, and "went forth, not knowing." I left it all, not because I wanted to, but because I had to.

I wish I could take credit for having enough faith, courage, and foresight to have chosen all this as logically and sensibly as it now seems in the telling. The truth is, most of it was a forced march in front of a gun barrel called circumstance; that is, what I did was the consequence of what I was becoming. I could not have done it differently then. Nor would I choose to do it differently now.

That God was in the process I do not doubt. I see his fingerprints all over the place.

That is not to say that the process was without pain. I feel it now even as I write about the experience. "Red" Smith, former sportswriter for the *New York Times*, had a simple formula for writing, "You just sit down and open up a vein." I don't know any other way to write a volume of self-disclosure.

In reading over the last few paragraphs, I see I've made the same mistake again. Self-justification is so easy to slip into. Everything I have said is true, but it is only half the truth. I come out looking lily white and clean as a hound's tooth. What I have shown you is my *persona*, not my shadow side, and that is an (unwitting) deception on my part.

The whole truth is that I am a mixture of light and shadow. I am both good and bad. Undoubtedly, I have acted with improper motivation in some circumstances, although I don't recall that it was ever with deliberate intent. I am very capable of being petty also. I am certain that I harbored hurt feelings for an unnecessarily long time. I was unable to hold together a marriage of thirty-five years. How much of it was my fault? Who can say? To reply "A lot," may not be very precise, but is probably quite accurate.

If it were not for a total reliance on grace, my absorption with guilt would have me beating my breast and confessing *mea culpa* for the rest of my days.

Thank God for grace!

For a while my life and career were in shambles. Yet I had a vibrant sense of freedom that wanted to express itself in dancing, not an elegant ballroom dance, but the fiery, passionate dance of Zorba the Greek.

Zorba danced when he was happy, and he danced when he was sad. When his three-year-old son was dying, all were weeping except Zorba; he expressed his sorrow in dance. "It was the dancing, only the dancing, that stopped the pain," he explained.

Zorba teams up with a practical, stolid English businessman. He is so pleased with their partnership that he must express his feelings or burst.

"Boss, do you dance?" Zorba asks.

"No."

"Then get out of the way. I may knock you down," and he twirls and twists and turns until he collapses.

They invest all their capital in a rig to get trees down a mountain to the sea. But on the trial run, the whole thing collapses, leaving both partners penniless.

As the splintered trees come careening down the mountain, the invited spectators flee in terror. Zorba and the passionless Britisher sit down alone in the middle of the debacle. They open a keg of wine and as they drink to each other's health, Zorba says affectionately, "Boss, you've got everything except a little madness. Every man needs a little madness."

Then he starts to laugh. It begins as a low chuckle and finishes in a gale of self-amusement: "Hey, boss, did you ever see a more splendiferous crash?" So infectious is he that the Englishman starts to laugh. They fall into each other's arms, out of breath with hilarity.

His heart strangely moved, the careful, conforming Englishman looks at Zorba and says longingly, "Teach me to dance."

It is a touching moment, pregnant with hope.

Sitting amid the shattered pieces of my life, that was my cry to God. Visceral. Primeval. "Teach me to dance!"

To dance? My circumstances argued the implausibility while my background reinforced the impossibility of it.

I am still awed that it happened at all. But even more, I am amused that as the new wine bubbled out of the fissures in the old wineskin, my dance began in that most incongruous of all places—on the strait and narrow.

AUTHOR'S NOTE: For the purposes of this volume, I have chosen to stay with the King James Version spelling of *strait* even though the useage is archaic. Meaning "narrow and constricted," the original spelling was *streit*, from Old French *estreit* (tight, narrow) from Latin *strictus* (to draw tight). The biblical meaning is not served by the word *straight*, meaning "without curve."

Introduction

"Why is it that you theologians seem to give less attention to Jesus than you do to the apostle Paul?" I asked my friend, a professor in a European seminary. I knew the question was loaded, laced with hyberbole, but I wanted to hear what he would say.

He thought for a moment and then agreed that I did have a point. He hadn't been consciously aware of it, he said, but it was true that he felt more comfortable with Paul than with Jesus. Paul was so logical in his arguments, so systematic in his style, so rational in his thinking. As a professor, my friend said, he needed a structured, organized approach to religious faith.

By contrast, Jesus was so, well, messy. It was easier to fit a professor's kind of thinking into Paul's carefully reasoned theological framework, he said, than to try and find one's way through the ambiguities and verbal mazes of the teachings of Jesus. He thought maybe that was why people in his profession tracked in a straight line with Paul instead of jumping around theological hopscotch squares with Jesus.

It made sense to me. More than once I have quickly passed over something Jesus said because it was too perplexing to figure out. We agreed, the professor and I, that you can't put Jesus in a neat and tidy box. He told stories and left the loose ends dangling, as if to say, "You figure it out." There are lots of hard sayings of Jesus that I couldn't or wouldn't figure out still lying on the pages of my Bible.

He left contradictory statements unresolved. It's confusing when Jesus tells his followers, "Whoever does not have a sword must sell his coat and buy one," (Luke 22:36, TEV), and then a few hours later scolds Peter when he tries to protect him, "Put your sword back in its place. . . . All who take the sword will die by the sword" Matt. 26:52, TEV).

Moreover, Jesus' way of life was certainly unconventional for a religious teacher. Unlike the separatist Pharisees, he was a socializer, who ate, drank, laughed and publicly enjoyed himself at parties in the homes of identifiable sinners. His style was at the other end of the pole from that of his ascetic cousin John. Yet Jesus praised the stern prophet of the wilderness by saying none in the kingdom was greater than he.

What he did and said must be very perplexing to anyone who needs clear rules of conduct and behavior, upsetting especially those Christians who think that ethics and morals are what the Church is about. If ethics and morals are the primary products of the Church, then we'd best franchise the whole operation out to the Buddhists, who've got a pretty good line of goods themselves ready to market in the same territory.

And please tell me what practical help in selecting allies and friends are these two conflicting criteria: "He who is not with me is against me" (Matt. 12:30) and "For he who is not against us is for us" (Mark 9:40)?

Taken separately, each is a categorical statement. Put them together, and they compound confusion. Which verse do I apply when starting or evaluating a relationship? And under what circumstances? Could it be that those are the very questions Jesus wants me to keep asking, so I can get daily guidance from the Holy Spirit? The unsafe and unsatisfying alternative, it seems to me, is to mechanistically drag out a proof text every time I'm required to assess a new situation.

Then there's the crafty manager Jesus approvingly told about (Luke 16:1–8) whose master praised him for arranging a comfortable retirement for himself by manipulating the books. Where does he fit into your understanding of honesty and integrity? That's one I pass in the fast lane because it still blows all my circuits.

Don't look for a straight-line answer. The whole business is, well, quite messy.

Does that make Jesus a sloppy thinker, a bad theologian, or a poor communicator? Only to our neat and orderly Western minds, held in thrall as they are by the ancient Greek philosophers. That's where we got the basis for our Western logic, with its rigid categories and polarized definitions. Aristotle told us that A can never be non-A, that black and white shall never meet, and that *gray* is a four-letter word. Today, millions of people who don't know Aristotle from Archimedes still bow before his shrine of black-and-white thinking.

But Jesus was not a Greek. He was from the Middle East, born on the bridge between the cultures of East and West, and he never traveled beyond the borders of his homeland. On one side of that bridge, Eastern philosophies have always been able to tolerate apparent contradictions and ambiguities, holding them in delicate balance. The Chinese, for instance, aren't just playing semantic games when they say, "A is right, and B is not wrong." They know about contradictory truths and how to hold them in creative tension.

However, conflicting ideas left unresolved offend our Western sense of orderliness. In part, at least, this was the basis of some of the great disputes in the early Church, which led to shattering schism. Driven by the high motivation of protecting the divinity of Jesus, a fourth-century bishop named Arius said that he could not possibly have been fully human—a little bit, maybe, but it was mostly celestial sleight of hand; God did it with mirrors. So conjuring up a little magic of his own, Arius made Jesus a kind of cosmic role player, an extraterrestrial come to earth, more than man but less than God.

Apparently Arius and his disciples reasoned that since A can never be non-A, it was against all human logic to say that Jesus was 100 percent man while at the same time 100 percent God. This is what the church fathers debated in A.D. 325, at the Council of Nicaea, where they adopted wording in the creed declaring the Son to be of "one substance" with the Father, a rather momentous anti-Arian phrase.

Oh yes, and the rest of the bishops threw out the blasphemers. But if the heretics were wrong in their theology, they were right on at least two other counts: first, the truth as the Nicene Creed stated it was contradictory, and second, it flouted human logic.

There are those infuriating loose ends again, left dangling all over the place. Terribly untidy.

When reading the Sermon on the Mount, it is helpful to remember that Jesus was not only the Son of God, he was also a son of his times. He was divine and human, with no tricky trapdoor in his personality to move back and forth between his two natures. As fully man, his teachings, his style all reflected his culture and his place.

Paul, too, was a son of David, but he was a Jew deeply influenced by Greek thought because of his upbringing. Probably no one understood the mind of Jesus better than Paul. Those years in the Arabian desert learning theology under the tutelage of the Author of the Textbook uniquely qualified Paul to synthesize the life and message of Jesus, giving them structure and coherence. Under his pen, they made sense to the Western mind.

But Jesus had a different set of priorities. He lived each encounter on the basis of its impact on human life, not whether it would look neat and tidy when it was put down on paper. In fact, the only record of Jesus writing at all was when he wrote something on the ground for the eyes of the Pharisees who wanted to stone the adulterous woman, obviously an existential footnote not intended to be carried over into history.

Jesus was more concerned with principles than with dogma, and such persons often appear inconsistent to law-and-order types. For principled people, each situation requires evaluation. Rules are not ignored or negated, but they must be weighed in the balance against principles.

For example, because rules are necessary to regulate society, legislatures set speed limits. The principle behind the law is the protection of life on the highways. The rule is a prescribed safe speed. But what happens when the rule and the principle collide, for example, when a private car violates the limit while rushing a heart attack victim to the hospital? What happens is an inconsistent action; that is, the law is broken, by an otherwise law-abiding citizen, to save a life.

The contradictory action (speeding) is completely consonant

with the overarching principle (protecting life), even though it technically violates the law. Jesus said as much when he defended his disciples' gathering grain on the Sabbath to meet their need for food. The religious leaders accused them of breaking the law by working on the Sabbath. But Jesus said, in so many words, "You simply don't understand the higher principle. The Sabbath was made for human beings, not vice versa. What incredible moral contortionists you are, straining at a gnat and swallowing a camel!"

That was the substance of the conflict between Jesus and the Pharisees. The principles he taught the common people conflicted with the behavior demanded by these authorities. In *The Parables of the Kingdom,* Robert Farrar Capon puts it in a nutshell: "To judge from the responses Jesus provoked from the religious experts of his day, it is plain that what he said and did didn't look much like religion to them. Respectable religionists can spot an absence of conventional piety a mile away, and the scribes and Pharisees did just that."[1] Their knee-jerk reaction was, if nothing else, consistent, for they rejected both the Teacher and his teachings.

But for us it is more difficult. Our faith won't allow us to throw out either baby or bath water. But neither will our bureaucratic instinct for conformity allow us to comfortably accommodate such a patchwork theology. It's enough to make a Pharisee rend his robe! All we want is for Jesus to make rational sense. So we help him out by mucking around with his stories and teachings, trying to harmonize the perceived discrepancies through our countless commentaries and eternal exegeses. Our tidy minds have got to fit them into a logical framework because we don't know how to hold them in creative tension.

We're no better at it than were the Pharisees—or the early church, which didn't handle the new freedom very well either. They wanted to keep the old wineskin of legalistic Judaism but decorate it with Christian symbols.

Little wonder that with our passion for dogma, we went a step further and turned the Sermon on the Mount into a new set of rules—tougher than the Ten Commandments, lots tougher. And why not? Our New Testament faith, the argument goes, should have standards even more demanding than the Old Testament standards. It was given to us, after all, in the light of full, not partial, revelation. God was no longer hiding in crevasses and clouds. In Jesus, we have the "fullness of the Godhead bodily." Being here in the person of his Son, God no longer had to write on stone tablets with a laser finger.

It's all so terribly logical, so transparently sensible, isn't it? In the words of Brennan Manning: "How blessed are the sensible men; they shall see the very tip of their noses."[2]

So we made the mount of the sermon into our New Testament Sinai. And Jesus became not the fulfillment of the law, but the new Lawgiver.

We got a new legalism, complete with rules and regulations, to say nothing of a new breed of self-anointed enforcers who make the Pharisees look like paragons of charity. How could we possibly have ended up with this monstrous distortion? It wasn't hard: somebody felt that Christians needed rules to supplement the Holy Spirit's guidance in ordering their ethical conduct, and somebody else thought the Church needed rules to justify its continuity as the guardian of something or other. Neither came close to doing what Jesus had in mind. He tried to tell us that our experience with the Father was a relationship, not a transaction, that love affairs don't require rules to flourish, that passion thrives in freedom, and that strictures are like a killing frost.

In the Sermon on the Mount, Jesus is not laying a new legalism on us. Instead, he shows us the principles behind the existing code of ethical conduct (much of which is found in cultures outside the Hebraic, incidentally), and suggests that we live by the principles rather than by the frosty rules. The letter kills, but the Spirit gives life.

A love affair reduced to numbers is about as exciting as an algebraic formula. Faith by the numbers is no better. Color it prosaic, humdrum, dead. But that's what you get when you try to quantify a living relationship. For my money, I'll take the Song of

Solomon with its burning sense of passion and possession any day. I am more stirred by what the Lover's heart feels than what his head thinks.

When we finished transforming our spiritual relationship with the Father into a religious transaction, we not only had eliminated the passion, we also had lost the mystery.

That is the saddest thing of all. The mystery is gone. We gave it up when we tried to make the divine understandable. If God would allow Moses at Sinai to see only his back, what incredible chutzpah possesses us to try and illuminate him fully, leaving nothing in the shadows?

God is mystery. Life is mystery. Incarnation is mystery. Redemption is mystery. And we need mystery. It is true that our physical survival demands a visible means of support, but emotionally, we require an *in*visible one as well. We need it because life's essential realities are beyond rational explanation. A mystery is no less real merely because it cannot be put on a slide under a microscope, brought into focus through a telescope or explained by a mathematical formula.

In *The Kingdom Within*, John Sanford points out, "The demons and angels, principalities and powers, dreams and visions which throng the pages of the New Testament bear testimony to the conviction of the early Christians that man's conscious life was immersed in a sea of spiritual reality."[3]

This belief in the transcending importance of the inner world energized the Church in the early centuries. Today we keep wanting to define reality only in terms of what our senses can experience, discounting any evidence of reality that is not empirical.

It is imperative that we relight the lamp of mystery on the altars in our hearts; without it we're left with a black void. Because nature abhors a vacuum, we search for something to fill what the French philosopher Blaise Pascal called the "God-shaped vacuum" inside us. Satan understands full well the necessity of mystery in human life. When religious systems start to demythologize the faith, he has a full inventory of counterfeits that he pulls out to fill the void.

The latest deception Satan has dusted off and refurbished is called "trance channeling," using voices from the netherworld to communicate through human mediums à la the new metaphysical fad promoted by Shirley MacLaine and other New Age gurus. Nothing about it is new; only the names have been changed to protect the guilty. Threadbare and phony as they are, channeling and reincarnation and swamis and yogis and karma and all the rest meet the human need for mystery.

At a time when the yuppie generation feels trapped in a highly rationalized and technological society that offers only spiritual emptiness, the Church has failed them by dispensing a demythologized faith. In spite of its cultlike beliefs, many of these intelligent and affluent young adults have embraced the New Age. They don't seem to have a problem handling mystery. Too bad the Church does.

Maybe we should resurrect William of Ockham—or at least his ideas. He was a fourteenth-century Franciscan philosopher who said, and I paraphrase him, "Why invent a new mystery to explain an old one?" Since Latin was the scholarly language of his day, what he actually said was, *"Non sunt multiplicanda entia praeter necessitatem,"* that is, "Entities are not to be multiplied beyond necessity." In other words, the simplest explanation that satisfies the conditions of the problem is the best. He employed this principle so often, so effectively, and so sharply to cut through the philosophical fog of his day that it came to be known as Ockham's razor.

Viewing the present situation, probably Ockham would say, "Since we already have such a corking good mystery in the entire Creator/creature relationship, let's exploit that one rather than leave room for a counterfeit."[11]

We don't need another mystery! Why can't we allow God to play peekaboo with his world, showing us a fingerprint here and there without revealing any more of the mystery than he has already unveiled in Jesus? Let him be, if he chooses, the divine Yeti, who will not satisfy our curiosity with anything more than a God-sized footprint in the snow or an eternal shape disappearing in the swirling mountain mists.

Spare us, please, any more demythologizing from the right and from the left. Already Jesus' friends at both ends of the theological spectrum have made him too definitive, too scrutable, too ordinary. They can tell you without any hesitation what position Jesus would take on every issue and exactly what he would do in every circumstance. Piffle and poppycock! Even his disciples, who walked the dusty roads with him every day, were constantly surprised at his unpredictable responses. Jesus was always in conflict with custom and convention. And there he stands—the Incomparable One, the same yesterday, today, and forever, the mystery of God incarnate in a human body. Absolutely mind-boggling!

If Christians on the right will quit dressing up Jesus in a three-piece suit and parading him around Washington as an endorsement for their favorite crusades, and Christians on the left will stop trying to make him the consummate revolutionary, we just might recover the mystery inherent in his Person. That holy mystery would add a terribly exciting dimension to our faith.

An old definition says that theology is "the science of God and things divine." But what we have been given is not a scientific formula; it is a living relationship. The Sermon on the Mount is not transactional theology in which we somehow bind God to keep all his promises by vowing to keep all his rules.

In fact, the Sermon on the Mount is not normative at all. If it is, what do you do with all that business of turning the other cheek and giving away your coat and plucking out your offending eye and cutting off your hand? If you try to make the Sermon on the Mount into a standard of conduct and aren't completely consistent in every point, you have torpedoed your own argument. Ready to give up now?

Then let it be what it is—descriptive. It is a picture of what life can be like for Kingdom people who take the risk of living by principles instead of accepting slavery to a set of rules. That is the high ground where it belongs.

Don't try to make the Sermon on the Mount a guide book for ethical living, either. It is deep calling unto deep, the depth of God whispering to the depth of our inner reality, suggesting that this is what life was meant to be. Life on the strait and narrow is a grand and glorious mystery, an audacious adventure. The materialists want to rationalize it away. The legalists want to put a fence around it. Both would destroy the mystery, leaving us to look for another one to satisfy the need of our barren souls. Why multiply entities unnecessarily? Remember? Bring back Ockham's razor!

As we touch the edges of the Sermon on the Mount, I hope you are able to see the sweep and scope of it, feel the glory and grandeur of it, hear the music of it, dance to the beat of it. It's OK to count when you are first learning to dance—one, two, three, and one, two, three, and so on—but finally you'd better get your mind off your feet and the numbers and go with the rhythm and romance of being in the arms of your beloved.

When you let the experience carry you along, you'll understand the difference between dancing and moving your feet. And believe me, there is a difference.

What's it like to forget the numbers, give your feet over in gay abandon, and go dancing with Jesus on the strait and narrow? It's certainly not dull, wearisome and melancholic. Nobody ever accused him of that. If you believe his critics, you might find him irreverent, illogical, inconsistent, and impertinent. But when you're in the arms of the Beloved, somehow that all becomes irrelevant.

Caught up in the freedom of this superlative experience of grace, you'll find it exciting, entrancing, intoxicating. And if by this time you are sufficiently liberated, you might hear yourself expressing the inexpressible in this paean of joy from Celia, one of Shakespeare's most uninhibited and delightful characters in *As You Like It*: "Oh, wonderful, wonderful, and most wonderful and yet again wonderful and after that out of all whooping."

Oh, yes, whoop it up, and dance on! You might shake up the Establishment, but Kingdom pilgrims will understand.

1. Call to the Radical Life

A word of warning.

The dance is not a sleepy waltz.

The beat of the music is not the Muzak that flows out of speakers in office buildings and elevators. Oh, no. This music throbs with life, vitality, animation, energy.

For pulse-racing rhythm and flaming rhetoric, absolutely nothing tops the Sermon on the Mount. Don't be misled by our soft interpretations of such big-time stuff as the Beatitudes and the Lord's Prayer. We come to the Sermon on the Mount with kid gloves on lined with asbestos because it's hot, too hot to handle. Some of it is downright revolutionary.

Compared with Jesus, many of the most luminous names in the history of revolution—Karl Marx, Mao Tse-tung, or even Thomas Jefferson—come off as being downright wimpish.

The Sermon on the Mount provides the beat for the dance. It is Jesus' call to the radical life, going as it does to the root of issues and relationships. It is fundamental and foundational, drastic and extreme, imperative and essential, superlative and transcending.

Anyone who glibly says, "Oh, I'm not very religious, but I try to live by the Sermon the Mount," doesn't have the slightest idea what it's all about. Probably someone like that is thinking vaguely of what we call the Golden Rule, "Do unto others as you would have them do unto you."

That's in the Sermon on the Mount, right enough. But to believe that one maxim is the sum total of one's spiritual obligation is roughly the equivalent of counting the stars that can be seen with the naked eye and delaring that you have counted all the stars in the heavens. Ever since Galileo invented the telescope, we've known there's more up there than meets the eye.

An astronomer who was on his way to give a lecture discovered that his seatmate on the airplane was a preacher. Early in the conversation he assured the clergyman that he knew everything about religion he needed to know. The preacher expressed delight and asked where the scientist had studied religion and how much he had read the Bible.

"Oh, no," the astronomer replied, "I've never studied theology, and I don't read the Bible, but I know the Golden Rule, and I figure that's enough religion for me."

"Well, on that basis," declared the preacher, "I guess I know all about astronomy."

The scientist scoffed and asked the pastor what he knew about the cosmos. To which the man of the cloth replied gravely, "Twinkle, twinkle little star; how I wonder what you are."

The Sermon the Mount as we have it in Matthew 5–7 is Jesus' attempt to take us back to basics. He wants us to discover our spiritual roots. It is a perplexing, disturbing, and dangerous body of teaching. The most common danger, I have discovered, is that the moment I accept a superficial and comfortable interpretation of one of Jesus' teachings, I immediately discover a troubling contradiction that defies my attempts to resolve it by logic and reason.

It is then I am forced to admit that some parts of the Sermon seem almost too tough to handle. Yet experience confirms my conviction that in these words, spoken shortly after his baptism, Jesus is laying out the principles of life that alone can bring liberation of personality, fullness of spirit, and superlative happiness. The Sermon on the Mount is the musical score that provides the beat for the dance of life.

I know that seems to fly in the face of Jesus' introduction to the strait and narrow. On first reading—even on the second and third reading, for that matter—it sounds downright harsh and forbidding: "Enter by the narrow gate; for the gate is wide, and the way is broad that leads to destruction, and many are those who enter by it. For the gate is small, and the way is narrow that leads to life, and few are those who find it" (Matt. 7:13–14, NASB). That hardly resonates with happiness, freedom, and joy.

But the reason this passage seems harsh is that we have already selected synonyms for "strait" and "narrow." We are sure Jesus meant "austere and limiting." With that predisposition, how could we interpret this teaching except in a legalistic and restrictive way? We are convinced that Jesus, acting like some scowling, celestial killjoy, is determined to take all the fun out of life.

The truth, however, is 180 degrees in the other direction. Jesus is telling us that only on the strait and narrow can life be lived in true freedom and unbounded joy. A contemporary paraphrase of those verses by Ben Campbell Johnson unlocks their true meaning:

> Choose God's way and give it priority in your life because there are many easy choices you can make which will lead to meaninglessness and despair, and many persons will choose those routes. Because the choice to express the Spirit dimension requires you to focus your life and bring it under control, few people will choose it. They would rather keep all their options open, a course which results in the loss of life and meaning.[1]

I used to have the idea that the strait and narrow was an obscure path that ran alongside and parallel to the broad road that Jesus spoke about. The broad road, I thought, was like an automobile freeway filled with fun-loving people rushing merrily to destruction. Meanwhile, a few sad-faced stragglers trudged the constricted path to heaven, casting scornful glances at the other crowd while trying to hide their envy behind masks of disapproval.

I was mistaken. The narrow way is not parallel to, but right smack in the middle of, the broad stream of humanity. The difference is that all the traffic on it flows in the opposite direction. The pilgrims journeying toward heaven are joyously dancing to the music of the redeemed. The masses traveling away from life contort their bodies in frenetic gyrations, but it isn't "the Dance," because they just aren't able to hear the music.

Ralph Waldo Emerson spoke a great truth about this path when he said, "Where you are on the path is not nearly as important as the direction you are facing." In other words, direction is more important than distance.

The reason the path is described as narrow is not that Jesus takes all the fun away, but that to find it we must focus our life.

This means making choices and establishing priorities. Most of us arrive at the gateway to God's Kingdom with all kinds of accumulated baggage under each arm that just cannot be accommodated by a narrow passageway. Something's got to go, and we have to decide which pieces of excess baggage to jettison. Hopefully, in the selection process, we will toss out discredited beliefs, destructive prejudices, and distorted values. There's no room for negative things. They've got to go.

But when Paul became a Kingdom person, he didn't stop at discarding just the bad things. He understood the axiom "The good is the enemy of the best." Even things that were not necessarily bad *per se* had to be cast aside in order to concentrate on Kingdom priorities: "I count everything sheer loss, because all is far outweighed by the gain of knowing Christ Jesus my Lord, for whose sake I did in fact lose everything" (Phil. 3:8, NEB).

Let's sum it up this way: Saying yes to Christ means saying no to other things so that we can be true to the yes.

The strait and narrow requires us to be selective rather than inclusive. For example, a commitment to be a concert pianist means not being able to be some other things, a baseball star, for instance. To excel as a downhill racer probably means not being able to become a gourmet chef. A commitment to do these things is "strait," like the entry point to Kingdom living, because it requires discipline and choices.

Igor Gorin, the Ukrainian-American baritone, tells of his early days of studying voice. He loved to smoke a pipe, but one day his professor said, "Igor, you will have to make up your mind whether you are going to be a great singer or a great pipe smoker. You cannot be both."

So the pipe went.

The difference between the narrow way and the broad way is the difference between a river and a swamp, between a laser beam and a floodlight. The power and force of the river and the laser are in sharp contrast to the undefined and nebulous character of the swamp and the floodlight.

What Jesus is telling us in the Sermon on the Mount is that life lived on any other terms is futile and empty. It has no cutting edge. Jesus barrels straight through the legalisms of established religions and gets to the principles of life that alone give meaning and fulfillment.

The gate is indeed narrow, because it can be found only by making selective choices. But the small gate opens up into the satisfying and abundant life that Jesus promises.

David described the experience in very picturesque language: "He reached down from on high and took hold of me; he drew me out of deep waters . . . [and] brought me out into a spacious place" (Ps. 18:16, 19, NIV).

What does the psalmist's word say to you? To me, it affirms that the strait and narrow is not a stifling prison cell (although I know some Christians who would prefer that kind of tight security and regimentation because they find the freedom of the Kingdom too threatening). But prison is what Jesus delivers us from, as Paul describes our liberation: "For ye have not received the spirit of bondage again to fear; but ye have received the Spirit of adoption" (Rom. 8:15, KJV).

When Jesus came, man-made rules and religious traditions had put the people in terrible spiritual bondage. There was no music to dance to. Life could never be happy, joyous, and free, because every normal activity was structured by a string of prohibitions. Traditions regulated all personal behavior and social intercourse, and Temple spies abounded who would report the slightest infraction. With all this emphasis on the negative, the religious teachers missed the underlying principles that gave the law meaning.

They inspected the trees with microscopic intensity, but never saw the beauty of the forest. They studied the letter of the Law, but gave no thought to the spirit that energized the principles. Jesus had scathing words for those teachers responsible for this spiritual slavery. Hypocrites and snakes, he called them. "They make up heavy packs and pile them on men's shoulders," he charged, "but will not raise a finger to lift the load themselves" (Matt. 23:4, NEB).

God had started out the human family with a handful of fairly simple regulations comprehensive enough to regulate life and most relationships. He put them in the heart of his creation long before he wrote them on stone tablets. The tablet business was just to formalize them so that as society became more complex the people wouldn't forget them.

Abba Eban, a former foreign minister of Israel, used to tell a story about Moses coming down from Mount Sinai and announcing, "There are twenty commandments."

The people respond, "Twenty commandments! You mean twenty 'Don't do this' and 'Don't do that'? Impossible! You've got to go back up there and get them revised."

So Moses went back up the mountain, and after forty days and forty nights he came down again and said, "I've got good news and I've got bad news. The good news is that God agreed to reduce the number to ten. The bad news is that he insisted on leaving in the one about adultery."

Relax. It's OK to chuckle, but it's also OK not to if the story is offensive. The point is this: God wasn't just trying to keep people from having fun. The seventh commandment is in there—just as the other nine are—not because God was feeling a little bilious that day, but because each one is based on a solid relationship principle.

But when Jesus came as the Law's fulfillment, just about everybody had forgotten why the commandments had been given in the first place. The original ten that God gave to Moses had been expanded and amended over the generations until there were 613 rules and traditions—248 affirmative and 365 negative, to say nothing of the subpoints.

Here's an example of how bad things were. God had said, "Remember the Sabbath day to keep it holy." All he meant was that the human body is not a machine, that it needs regular recovery periods, and that life will work better if we work six days and rest one day—the same pattern God followed in creation. But by the time Jesus came, there were scores of traditions defining just what could and could not be done on the Sabbath. And don't think these traditions were merely suggestions. The Pharisees made sure they carried the force of law by attaching penalties for violating them.

One Sabbath, as Jesus and his disciples were walking through a wheat field, the disciples picked some heads of wheat and ate the grain. Immediately, Old Hawkeye, a Temple spy, accused them of profaning the holy day. In response, Jesus showed how inconsistent the man-made rules patched together by the Pharisees were. He reminded them that the Sabbath was made for our benefit; that was the reason God gave the rule in the first place. Human beings weren't created to serve the Sabbath (Mark 2:27).

It was that kind of silly interpretation that Jesus was trying to correct with his revolutionary teaching in the Sermon on the Mount. He wanted to clear away the clutter of the centuries and get back to the radical truth. Life's basic principles, which God was affirming in the Ten Commandments, had been completely obscured by legalistic tradition.

In doing this Jesus is a bit like the little boy who was sent to clean the horse barn. As he shoveled out the mounds of manure, he muttered, "There's got to be a pony in here someplace." Jesus is trying to help us find the pony, to discover the reality, to dig down to the radical truth.

When we understand that, his teachings in these chapters seem less severe and more life-affirming. He shows us that the strait and narrow offers us a liberated and joyous way to live. He doesn't do that by abolishing the laws of God, by tearing down the fences. The laws are valid. The fences protect us. What Jesus does is show us the principles behind the laws and tell us that life works best when we work in harmony with those principles and not against them.

Often we speak of "breaking the commandments." What we mean is that we violate them. We don't break them. Instead, if we persistently violate them, they break us.

Examples abound. Jesus cites the commandment, "You shall not kill," and then adds, "But I tell you, if anyone is unjustifiably angry with another person, he will have to face the consequences of his feelings. . . . And if anyone completely discounts another person, he is in danger of losing his own personhood" (Matt. 6:21–22)[2].

In other words, it is not just murder, but hatred and anger, harsh words and hostile feelings that are the heart conditions that must be dealt with. The prohibition against killing is more truly an affirmation of the positive principle of love and respect for all. If we live by any other standard, we cannot help but become broken persons.

Jesus also refers to the seventh commandment, the one that got former President Jimmy Carter (then candidate Carter) in trouble for his honesty in admitting in an interview that he had lusted: "You have heard that it was said, You shall not commit adultery. But I say to you, that every one who looks at a woman lustfully has committed adultery with her in his heart" (Matt. 5:27–28).

The attitude, Jesus says, is as important as the act. What Jesus is doing is affirming the marriage covenant between two people, which is violated by even an inner desire for immoral experiences. He is saying that, whether we believe it or not, life works best when two people live in fidelity to each other. Any other way leads to brokenness.

When Jesus talks about plucking out the offending eye or cutting off the delinquent hand, statements that perplex us all today, he is, as one writer says, "expressing in metaphorical language . . . that a limited but morally healthy life is better than a wider life which is morally depraved."[3]

We must agree, I think, that Jesus makes a lot of sense. The radical life to which he calls us is a sensible life. He calls us back to love of God and neighbor, back to respect for all persons, back to basic human values.

The entire Law, according to Jesus, rests on just two commandments. First, love God with all your heart, soul, mind, and strength. Second, love your neighbor as yourself. These form the root system out of which all other relationships grow.

The most radical kind of life imaginable is to live by the old-fashioned virtues of esteem, acceptance, love, honesty, decency, reverence, and tenderness. These are the principles behind the laws. To live by these is to be a Kingdom person. They will open the gateway to abundant and joyful living on the strait and narrow. They will liberate us from the tyranny of self-rule, and they will unlock the potential in our lives and in the lives of people we touch.

Father Brennan Manning, a Catholic priest, found such a Kingdom person at the lowest point in his life. He describes his encounter with a gentle and nonjudgmental man who found him on the floor of a cheap motel in a southern city, desperately sick and near death. Father Manning had barely managed to crawl to the telephone, dial "0" and ask the operator to call Alcoholics Anonymous.

Within ten minutes, a man he'd never seen walked in the door. Father Manning writes, "He had the Breath of the Father on his face and an immense reverence for my life. He scooped me up in his arms and raced me to a detox center."

The stranger stayed with him through the hell of withdrawal. "His words might sound corny to you, like tired old cliches. But they were words of life to me. . . . He told me the Father loved me, that He had not abandoned me. . . . Above all else, he affirmed me in my emptiness and loved me in my loneliness. Again and again he told me of the Father's love; how when his children stumble and fall, He does not scold them but scoops them up and comforts them. Later I learned that my benefactor was an intinerant laborer who showed up daily at Manpower, a local employment agency. He put cardboard in his work shoes to cover the holes.

"Yet, when I was able to eat, he bought me my first dinner at MacDonald's. For seven days and seven nights, he breathed life into me physically and spiritually and asked nothing in return. Later I learned that he had lost his family and fortune through drinking."

Father Manning recovered and moved on. Two years later, however, he was in the same town and called AA to locate his friend. Sadly he was told the man was back on Skid Row. He had been twelve-stepping too often. (The Twelfth Step in the AA program is to help other practicing alcoholics.) In one of life's tragic ironies, the man had burned himself out caring for others and gone back to the bottle.

As Father Manning drove through Skid Row, he thought he spotted his friend in a doorway. However, it turned out to be just another wino who, with hand trembling, reached out and said, "Hey, man, can you gimme a dollar to get some wine?"

"I knelt down before him," Father Manning continues, "and took his hands in mine. I looked into his eyes. They filled with tears. I leaned over and kissed his hands. He began to cry. He didn't want a dollar. He wanted what I wanted two years earlier lying on the motel floor—to be accepted in his brokenness, to be affirmed in his worthlessness, to be loved in his loneliness. He wanted to be relieved of what Mother Teresa of Calcutta, with her vast personal experience of human misery, says is the worst suffering of all—the feeling of not being accepted or wanted."

Father Manning never saw his friend, but he said that a few days later while he was celebrating the Eucharist for a group of recovering alcoholics, the man walked in the door. He didn't stay, but two days later the priest received a letter from him, which read in part, "'Two nights ago in my own clumsy way I prayed for the right to belong, just to belong among you at the holy Mass of Jesus. You will never know what you did for me last week on Skid Row. You didn't see me, but I saw you. When I saw you kneel down and kiss that wino's hands, you wiped away from my eyes the blank stare of the breathing dead. When I saw you really cared, my heart began to grow wings, small wings, feeble wings, but wings. I threw my bottle of Gallo wine down the sewer. Your tenderness and understanding breathed life into me, and I want you to know that. You released me from my shadowy world of panic, fear and self-hatred. God, what a lonely prison I was living in.'"[4]

That is radical living. Fundamental loving. Revolutionary caring. It makes no judgment, offers no sermons on ethics, establishes no hierarchy of righteousness. It simply accepts, affirms, heals.

That is what the Church ought to be about. It is the only unique thing we have to give to sinners who already feel condemnation, judgment and guilt. It is the lived-out experience of a Kingdom person who, when standing at the crossroads one day, chose the freedom and joy of the strait and narrow. It is the distilled essence of the Sermon on the Mount that expresses itself not in the letter of the Law, which numbs and kills, but in the liberty of the Spirit, which resurrects and makes alive.

The music swells.

The divine Drummer establishes the beat.

The dance of joy begins.

2. How Strait? How Narrow?

A lot of people belonging to my generation grew up in a religious environment that was negative and repressive. At least, I judge there are a lot of them, because I meet these spiritual kinfolk just about everywhere I go. Like me, they are trying to recover from the damage caused by a legalistic and judgmental gospel inflicted upon them early in life.

Looking back, I know now that this "bad news" interpretation of the good news had a lot more to do with community social standards and cultural mores than it did with biblical principles. Our daily spiritual life, as well as our position in Christ, were judged by peers more on the basis of what we didn't do than by what we did. Somebody described it in this piece of doggerel: "I don't smoke and I don't chew; I don't go with girls who do."

Actually, I didn't know any girls who chewed tobacco anyhow, and the handful who smoked in those days did so secretly. Some of their mothers did dip snuff, however, which was more acceptable for country women in the South.

In my rather bleak religious environment, to "get saved" virtually meant that you had to turn your back on life. The spiritual and the secular were carefully delineated, and born-again people were admonished to eschew what was popularly called "the world." We dumped into that category everything we were against.

I recall one pastor telling me that his church didn't believe in recreation programs for young people. Playing softball was "worldly." He wanted them only in spiritual programs, studying the Bible, he said. I think he truly believed that was all they did. Of course, I knew what happened when they left the church and took the long way home!

Dancing? Hoo, boy! That and movies ranked right up there as the twin biggies, virtually guaranteeing you a first-class seat in perdition. Of course, card playing was pretty high on the list, too, unless the game was Old Maid. In my world, we never talked about freedom and joy on the strait and narrow. Why should we? They were mutually exclusive. My early impression of the strait and narrow was that it was about as much fun as a case of the measles.

H. L. Mencken, noted author and perceptive interpreter of the human condition, described us rather well in his definition of a Puritan as a person who has a haunting fear that somebody, somewhere, is having a good time.

As a young man, I prayed Augustine's prayer of his youth, "Lord, save me, but not now." I was scared of the flames of hell as described by the tent evangelists who came through each summer, but at the same time I wanted to have some fun before putting on the hair shirt of salvation. I wished that I might know the exact day of my death so I could enjoy life right up to the day before and then settle my account with God by a deathbed repentance. I do admit, though, to having some anxiety that God might question the sincerity of such a premeditated last-minute confession.

Oh, wretched boy that I was! I wanted to love God, but I thought that getting religion meant saying no to life. If, as John Barrymore said, "Life is the curtain-raiser to the Big Show," I didn't want to miss the warm-up act either. I wanted to experience life, not be sewn up in some passionless cocoon until I could emerge as a sainted butterfly in heaven.

Now, many years later, I am convinced that among the first questions God will ask us when we meet him face to face is, "Did you enjoy my world? Did you have fun while you were there?" I'll tell him that I thought it was absolutely smashing!

Only much later did I become aware how gross my earlier distortions were. That insight came when I started studying the Sermon on the Mount, freed from those early perversions. It isn't important to me whether the Sermon on the Mount was spoken at one time in one place or if it is a compilation by Matthew and Luke from Jesus' various encounters with the crowds. Whichever it is, when I read those teachings I recognize the voice of authority, as did the common people of Jesus' day. If the Sermon on the Mount were the basis for a course of study in a college curriculum, it would be listed in the catalog as Life 101. What Jesus said in chapters 5 through 7 of Matthew can be read, like a college text-book, superficially or deeply. It can have a little impact on our lives or a lot, depending on how open we are to becoming King-dom people.

When Jesus introduces the strait and narrow, the very words are enough to blunt an average person's enthusiasm, especially if we are easily daunted. What kind of monastic cell is Jesus offering us? Just how strait is the gate and how narrow the way? What does Jesus allow and what does he disallow? And how much of our answer to these questions is shaped by our contemporary social and cultural standards rather than by the demands of Jesus?

First of all, let's clear up some misconceptions. The word that is translated "strait" is not the one we use when we talk about a straight line. Here, "s-t-r-a-i-t" does not mean without curve or deviation. So, don't be distressed if your life isn't a beeline to heaven. Actually, as Christian found out in John Bunyan's allegory *Pilgrim's Progress*, the path to the Eternal City has a lot of twists, turns, and detours.

"Strait," as Jesus uses it here, means narrow or constricted, confined or close. It's the same word used for straitjacket and straitlaced. This may be why we subconsciously, but erroneously, give it restrictive and puritanical connotations.

There is another misconception we need to explode. The road is not referred to as narrow because Jesus is a party pooper who takes all the fun out of life. It is some of the travelers who have given the road a bad reputation. If most conventional church peo-ple today can be described as "dismal, regular, and decent," words Huck Finn applied to the widow Douglas, it is not the fault of the road. Rather, it is a description of our own joyless and halfhearted experience.

Perhaps a more accurate translation of Jesus' words would read, "Narrow is the gate and *compressed* is the road." The compressed way runs in the opposite direction to the wide road, although parallel to it. The destination is life instead of death; it is, as Scott Peck titled his popular book, "the road less traveled."

The reason there is less traffic on the narrow way is that entering God's Kingdom through the "strait gate" requires that we limit our options, control our lives, strip down for action. But let's be clear about one thing. Though the strait and narrow gives us the opportunity to get life into focus, it doesn't take away our freedom.

An old spiritual says, "My Lord, it's so high you can't get over it; so low, you can't get under it; so wide, you can't get around it; you must come in at the door." In other words, there's no cheating our way into the Kingdom—Christ's new society. We enter into it by conscious choice when we are ready to pay the price. And a part of that price is bringing life under control and starting to limit our options.

There are times when narrowness may seem like vice, but often it can be a virtue. For example, a pilot who is bringing an airplane in for a landing works on a compass of 360 degrees, but the runway is laid out so there is only one heading that will bring the plane down safely. And, believe me, if I'm a passenger on that plane, I don't want a broad-minded pilot who decides to argue with the tower about the approach simply because he or she doesn't like the scenery. I want a pilot to limit the options, focus the instruments, and bring me safely down.

It is said that the noted pianist Paderewski would go over a single bar of music as many as forty times until he was sure he had mastered it. One day he played for Queen Victoria, who was deeply moved by his performance. In awe, she said, "Mr. Paderewski, you are a genius."

"That may be," he replied, "but before I was a genius I was a drudge."

That must have been a part of what was in the mind of Jesus when he said, "Strive to enter by the narrow door" (Luke 13:25). Striving is hard work, maybe even drudgery. Entering God's Kingdom requires effort. We won't accidentally stumble through the opening. The few who make it are those who passionately believe that achieving wholeness of life is worth the struggle. On the other hand, the crowd that travels the broad road is not alive to the indescribable joys of Kingdom living.

May I say it again? Focus is what it's all about. You must say no so you can say yes. Marriage requires the same exclusivity. When you say yes to your beloved, you must say no to all the other romantic interests in your life. Marriage demands the focus of love, and focus is what makes one way narrow and the other way broad. Let's go back to the metaphors I used in Chapter One—the river and the swamp, the laser and the floodlight. The river and the laser have enormous power. The river turns turbines and generates thousands of kilowatts of electric power. The laser cuts through steel. But a floodlight is nebulous and vague, and a swamp is sprawling and stagnant.

It is important at this point to understand, though, that Jesus never violates our freedom. He will not strong-arm us through the strait gate and onto the narrow way. The decision is ours, and it must emerge from an unsatisfied spiritual hunger. But if we listen, we will hear him encouraging us with the cryptic words, "He who has ears to hear, let him hear" (Matt. 11:15). I call it deep listening. A frivolous and superficial response just won't cut it.

Is it worth the effort? Think about it this way. What we give up are only things of lesser value in order to make room for things of infinitely greater worth. Jesus said, "The kingdom of heaven is like a merchant seeking fine pearls, and upon finding one pearl of great value, he went and sold all that he had, and bought it" (Matt. 13:45-46, ASV).

The jewel merchant wisely concentrates resources to acquire the finest pearl. The pilot rightly limits options in order to land safely. The concert pianist firmly establishes priorities to achieve success. The river keeps its direction focused so it can generate power.

Are these examples of limitations? They may seem so to a person who thinks that freedom means not having any discipline or control. But to the rest of us, restraints like these are chosen because they provide a welcome margin of safety.

But there's even more to be said. Journeying on the strait and narrow means that we can live creatively in the Spirit, not in conformity to religious and cultural traditions.

With penetrating insight Jesus in the Sermon the Mount dug beneath the accumulation of man-made traditions and revealed the spiritual principles that had been buried under centuries of cultural garbage. Most of the traditions were trivial, but they carried the weight of Holy Writ from Mount Sinai because the learned men and Pharisees said they should.

This burdensome code with its 613 points covered every possible human action and relationship. There was just no way a person could avoid breaking some of these traditions and laws. This simply meant that the religious authorities could arrest anybody at any time and try the culprit on some trumped-up charge, knowing that he or she couldn't help but be guilty of some infraction, even if it wasn't that particular one.

When Jesus healed a man on the Sabbath, the Pharisees started screaming about working on the designated day of rest. In response Jesus pointed out how absurd that was, since by their own law, it was permissible to perform an act of mercy, releasing an ox trapped in a ditch, for example, on the Sabbath. (Luke 14:5). But if you were just an ordinary person, you were no match for those crafty and suspicious minds whose full-time occupation was to find you guilty of something or other. They wanted to make you look bad, because the worse you looked, the better they looked. Oh, it was a cozy little moral scam.

Can you imagine, then, how astounded the common people must have been to hear Jesus say of those self-proclaimed paragons of virtue, "Unless your righteousness exceeds that of the scribes and Pharisees, you will never enter the kingdom of heaven" (Matt. 5:20).

How could anybody be more virtuous than the people who coined the definition of virtue and then wrote the rule book? No one kept more religious requirements than the scribes and Pharisees. Actually, that generation in the first century was not unlike our own. Then, many religious professionals talked a lot about faith but practiced and judged others by a religion based on works. Personal holiness was measured by externals, not by what was in the heart. Righteousness was behavioral rather than attitudinal, and goodness was calculated by the number of nice things you did and the number of bad things you didn't do.

If that sounds familiar, it should. We're still doing it today. Spirituality is still measured by the numbers, as if somehow we hope to gain God's approval by keeping the entries on the credit side of the ledger greater than those on the debit side. But there's not much freedom and joy in living by some kind of mathematical formula.

I love Martin Luther's shocking advice to his timid young student Melanchthon. "Love God, and sin boldly," the earthy Luther told him. He was not, as might seem on the surface, encouraging Melanchthon to do wrong. Luther was simply trying to free him from the pharisaical attitude that he could achieve holiness by a negative way of life.

Luther was saying, love God—that's the motivation—then live life fully and bravely as the sinner you are, trusting in God's grace. Since you can't earn one scintilla of spiritual virtue by your own merit, live zestfully and boldly while casting yourself on the mercy of God. Live creatively in the Spirit, allowing his freshness to blow through your soul, understanding that true righteousness is a depth morality of attitude and motive, not a numbered list of superficial dos and don'ts to be checked off.

There is no particular virtue in tradition—sentiment maybe, but no spiritual value. An attractive exterior is what we substitute when there is no spiritual beauty inside. When I see a church begin to focus on the externals—concentrating on rearranging its liturgy and form of worship, polishing its creed, tidying up its organizational structure, creating new committees, planning unnecessary buildings—I start sniffing around for dead men's bones. When there is no spiritual life inside either a church or a person, the first response is to whitewash the outside. That's what Jesus was getting at when he said, "Woe to you scribes and Pharisees, hypocrites! for you are like whitewashed tombs, which outwardly appear beautiful, but within they are full of dead men's bones and all uncleanness" (Matt. 22:27).

My experience is that the Holy Spirit is often messy and unpredictable specifically because he is dynamically alive, and we had best not try to control his work or repress his creativity. The Pharisees did, and look at what they ended up with: a neat, clean cemetery, planted with row upon row of tombstones to Tradition.

So Jesus came and offered us a strait gate and a narrow way that would take us out of the place of spiritual death into the celebration of life in the Kingdom of God.

Finally, the strait and narrow liberates us to live by the law of love as free persons, not prisoners in a locked cell of legalism. Am I saying there are no standards, no morality, no ethics in God's Kingdom? Not at all. In fact, Kingdom living requires a higher standard than legalism ever thought about. "Do not suppose that I have come to abolish the Law or the Prophets," Jesus said, "I did not come to abolish but to complete" (Matt. 5:17, NEB).

Completing, or perfecting, the Law meant revealing the higher principles on which each part of the code is based. The morality of Kingdom living is not established by rules imposed by an authority figure in some religious institution. That is legalism. Kingdom living is mandated by an inner motivation. Those who enter God's Kingdom by the strait gate find that the principles revealed in the Sermon on the Mount are the key to a life that is happy, joyous, and free. And the reason we continue to choose this higher morality is not that we fear the judgment of other people or the wrath of God, but that we want to experience more of this insanely rapturous life.

Sadly, many don't know that Jesus unlocked the prison when he came to set the captives free. A remarkable story is told about Harry Houdini, magician and escape artist, and even though it is disputed by some authorities on his life, it makes an important point.

Handcuffed and shackled, Houdini was placed in a London prison cell and given a short time to release himself. According to the story, he was out of the handcuffs and chains in a few minutes, but the lock on the cell door defied all his efforts to pick it. Dripping with sweat and exhausted, the famed magician sank to the floor of the cell and leaned against the door. It swung open freely— the jailer had left the door unlocked!

Few things can be more sad than spending our lives in a cell that Jesus has already unlocked.

In his book *Inside, Outside,* Herman Wouk has a significant story for Christians who are caught up in New Testament legalism. It is about David Goodkind, a young Jewish boy whose parents immigrated from Russia. David explains that his family was thoroughly Orthodox. They did everything properly. Not only did the family not eat pork, young David's mother never served meat and milk at the same meal, because it was against the code of Leviticus. Everything ingested had to be kosher.

For instance, drinking Coca-Cola was a very big deal. Not that there was something wrong with the drink itself—"The pious few," David says, "pointed out that the glue in the corks of Coca-Cola bottles could have come from horses; hence with your Coke you might consume a trace of an unkosher animal."

One day a rabbi came over from Russia and watched David's mother preparing food. With great seriousness, he advised her to use different cooking utensils for cooking meat and warming soup made from milk. So David's mother bought another pot. Then another rabbi came over, the most revered of them all. Zaideh told her that it was dangerous to dry the two pots with the same dish towel after you've cooked with them. So, she went out and bought two new dish towels—one with a red stripe and one with a blue stripe, so the the pots could be dried separately!

A few years later when David went off to study at the Talmudical Academy of Yeshiva University, all these rules learned from childhood had such a stranglehold on his life that he wasn't free to really love and know God. To him, God was a legalistic tyrant, not a loving Father.

At the academy, he says, "The pious ones and the rabbis did generate something pretty new to me: guilt, a scarlet thread which ran through yeshiva life."

But not through yeshiva life only. Guilt is the scourge used by most religious systems, not to bring us to God, but to horsewhip rebellious youngsters into line and produce conformity to tradition. The emotional scarring it leaves is often hideous and may well be one of the most violent forms of child abuse.

Troubled by the dish towel issue, David raises it with another student: "Will God strike me dead if I use the wrong dish towel? What's the point?"

The answer solemnly supports the system: "Once you start to compromise, the whole thing will break down. You have to stick to the rules."

But David is not satisfied. He meets an older student from his neighborhood who also has been deeply influenced by the system. He cannot leave the school, much as he would like to, because his father is a trustee. But he says with deep emotion to his younger friend: "Don't let it happen to you, Davey! Get out! Get away from this dish towel religion!"[1]

Orthodox Jews are not the only ones with a dish towel religion. Many Christians have one, too. They prefer to live by a rigid, legalistic code imposed from an outside source because in this complex and threatening world, freedom is too frightening. Having to make personal choices terrifies them, so they look for movements, authority figures, or proof texts that will tell them what is allowed or disallowed. It seems to me that is only a short distance from tarot cards and tea leaves, astrologers and fortune tellers. If things don't work out, blame it on fate.

Taking charge of their own lives is an option many people reject simply because they cannot bear the thought of having to shoulder all the blame when things go wrong. George Bernard Shaw understood this when he said, "Liberty means responsibility. That is why most men dread it."

A prisoner serving a life term in Texas for rape and murder expressed it this way, "I wouldn't trade places with those people on the outside for anything. In here, I don't have to think about anything—what time I'll get up or what I'll eat for the next meal. Every day is planned for me. Why would I want to trade that for the anxiety and worry outside these walls?"

Tragically, a prison can become bearable, even downright comfortable, if you stay there long enough.

In Byron's poem *The Prisoner of Chillon,* Bonnivard had been chained in the dungeon so long that he is ambivalent when freedom does come. He describes his feelings in these words:

> These heavy walls to me had grown
> A hermitage—and all my own. . . .
> My very chains and I grew friends,
> So much a long communion tends
> To make us what we are; —even I
> Regain'd my freedom with a sigh.

We don't have to choose it, but Jesus gives us the option of living as a free person by the law of love and every day making those excruciatingly wonderful decisions about what the loving thing to do is in a score of different circumstances.

Take it from one who has tried both ways to live—by the law of rules and by the law of love. With all the risks it entails, living by the law of love is better, infinitely better.

How strait is the gate and how narrow the way? Only strait enough to require that we leave behind our excess baggage and lesser priorities. Only narrow enough to demand that we focus our lives for power.

When I decided to live as a Kingdom person, the freedom and joy I experienced cannot be better described than in the words of Viktor Frankl. At a spiritual level, I understood what he must have felt when he walked out into a world without chains or bars after years in a concentration camp: "I walked through the country past flowering meadows, for miles and miles, toward the market town near the camp. Larks rose to the sky and I could hear their joyous song. There was no one to be seen for miles around; there was nothing but the wide earth and sky and the larks' jubilation and the freedom of space. I stopped, looked around, and up to the sky—and then I went down on my knees. At that moment there was very little I knew of myself or of the world—I had but one sentence in mind – always the same: 'I called to the Lord from my narrow prison and He answered me in the freedom of space.'"[2]

That's the answer to the questions, How strait? How narrow? As big as all outdoors! God liberates us from our self-made prison into the unshackled liberty of the Kingdom.

And gives us room to dance!

3. Loving Beyond the Boundaries

In the first century B.C., when Roman legions were going out to conquer and to expand the boundaries of the empire, mapmaking was a very inexact and rudimentary science. Not much was known about the world. Where knowledge ended and ignorance began, the symbols used on maps were dragons, sea monsters, and the like, indicating the dangers that were thought to lurk in those uncharted regions. One such ancient map carried the following legend on all uncharted regions: "Where leviathans and dragons be."

A story is told about a Roman battalion under the leadership of a particularly adventurous commander that found itself beyond the familiar landmarks known to the mapmakers. Not wanting to turn back, but apprehensive about pressing farther into unscouted territory, the commander dispatched a messenger to Rome with this urgent request, "Please send new instructions. We have marched off the map!"

In the Sermon on the Mount, Jesus does something like that. He leads us off the map of superficial spiritual and ethical practice into the uncharted lands of risky relationships. He takes us beyond the tight, safe boundaries of personal and social behavior—boundaries arbitrarily drawn and culturally approved by each new set of religious leaders, boundaries that offer comfort and security—and forces us to move into territory where he alone knows the way. And this new territory is known as the Kingdom of God.

That's one of the troubling things about Jesus. He's always leading us off the map. Just when I think I have learned the rules and mastered the system, when I start to feel comfortable with the "Thou shalts" and "Thou shalt nots," I find myself in the middle of some new experience for which the only signpost reads, "Perhaps."

Over and over again in the Sermon on the Mount, Jesus reminds the people, "You have heard that it was said of old . . ." and then repeats the teachings of the rabbis that for centuries had established the parameters of conventional conduct. But Jesus doesn't leave it there. He redraws those boundaries by introducing a new principle, a Kingdom teaching, prefaced by his words, "But I say to you . . ." And once again the beat changes, and we find Jesus leading the dancers across the border between the comfortable kingdom of Tradition and the radical Kingdom of God.

For example, the religious teachers had said, "You shall love your neighbor and hate your enemy" (Matt. 5:43). Well and good! That's what everybody did. It was perfectly normal human behavior, no mystery there. It was a manageable code of conduct that offered lots of room for self-congratulation, especially when we can decide who fits the classification "neighbor."

And then—whoops!—off the map I go as Jesus sweeps me beyond my comfort zone with the words, "But I say to you, Love your enemies and pray for those who persecute you, so that you may be sons of your Father who is in heaven" (Matt. 5:44–45). Suddenly, I am in a land of ethical behavior that no social topographer has yet mapped and where I dare proceed only with great courage and at great risk.

There beyond the boundaries, I must practice loving in the place of total vulnerability, where my fears tell me that dragons and monsters are waiting to devour me. The map brought me this far, but now I need to take the hand of the One who said, "I am the Way."

For those who are still under the illusion that the Sermon on the Mount is nothing more than a collection of pious sayings, I've got to point out that the admonition to love your enemies is hardly a platitude. It is a big principle, a major proposition, a hot potato to handle—maybe the hottest of all.

What does Jesus mean when he says that we are to love our enemies "so that you may be sons of your Father who is in heaven"? Does he mean that we aren't one of God's children when we don't love our enemies? Hardly, since faith alone, not our own goodness, no matter how great, is the only way to get into God's family.

That troubling statement is better translated this way, "Love your enemies . . . so that you may be a reflection of the mind and spirit of God" or "so that you may demonstrate the family characteristics of your Father." When we love our enemies, when we practice loving beyond the boundaries, we are acting out on earth the life and will of God, our Father in heaven.

"Love your enemies" is a hard saying when I stop idealizing it and begin making it practical. That means I have to love Pol Pot, the former tyrant of Cambodia who is responsible for the death of some of the dearest friends I had on this earth. I confess I don't want to love him, and I don't know how to start loving him. I also must love the communist ruler of Ethiopia, Mengistu, who I believe ordered the murder of the gentle, if ineffective, emperor Haile Selassie, whom I knew. Mengistu has thrown into prison thousands of Christian believers, some of whom were my friends.

And coming closer to home, I've got to love those notable Christian leaders whom I feel took advantage of my emotional devastation at a time of crisis in my life to protect their own images and settle some personal scores. That is a great struggle for me.

Who are the enemies you have to love? The scab who crossed your union picket line or the company president who refused to bargain in good faith? The husband who punched you? The friend you trusted who sold you out? The woman in the PTA who told lies about you? The family member who betrayed your trust?

We must love our enemies, whoever they are, because the alternative is to hate them, and hate is the antithesis of the character of our heavenly Father whose image we bear. It may be difficult to love our enemies, but it is not impossible, for loving is not accidental. It is not so much an emotion we feel as something we do. It is not some esoteric manifestation as much as some very mundane actions. To love lies within the power of the human will, and that is why Jesus gives it as a command rather than a suggestion.

In practical terms, what does it mean to love beyond the boundaries?

For one thing, it means loving inclusively, not selectively. That is the character and nature of our Father whose image we are supposed to reflect. Jesus says God "makes his sun to rise on the evil and the good, and sends rain on the just and on the unjust" (Matt. 5:45). The verbs *makes* and *sends* are action verbs. It is not just happenstance. God wills the sun and the rain for those who reject him as much as for his friends who accept him.

Jesus says our love is to be just that big and bold and non-discriminatory. *Strait* and *narrow* are adjectives that apply to the gateway to God's Kingdom and the pathway of the Christian pilgrim. They are not meant to circumscribe the quality and dimensions of our love.

But have you noticed the variety of techniques we devise to restrict our love to the congenial, the friendly, the lovable? A very popular one is something I call labeling. We attach a label to everybody—social, regional, racial, political, theological, denominational and so on *ad infinitum, ad nauseam*. And the label becomes the basis for approval or disapproval, for acceptance or rejection.

If you happen to be in one of the categories I like, that gains you my favor. But if I stick on you a pejorative label, then you don't qualify for my love and acceptance. And it's a very arbitrary system. You don't even have to know me in order to wear my label. When Richard Nixon was in the White House, he had his staff keep an enemies list. Those who were on it weren't even aware they carried that dubious distinction.

A few years ago, a woman lawyer from the upper Midwest wrote a book in which she accused me of belonging to, or at least consciously supporting, something called the New Age movement, which she said was a nebulous anti-Christian conspiracy. The most bizarre thing about the whole episode was that I had never heard of the movement, the woman, or the book until I was called by a radio station and asked about it. By that time she was making her wild charges in rallies around the country and cleaning up at the book stall afterward.

I was a victim of the labeling technique, not the first one and certainly not the last. Labels are so easy to attach, and they are so effective in allowing us to be selective about the people we will love.

I have observed that we start applying labels when we are afraid that some "unworthy" person may sneak under the umbrella of our love. After the labels are applied, we refine the categories even more to make sure the undeserving are kept out. There was a time when we generally agreed that anybody who called him- or herself a Christian would be accepted in our circle of love. But as we began to define the categories more narrowly, that didn't seem quite adequate, so we added "born-again." And when that gained general approval, we narrowed it with "Bible-believing." That was followed by "Christ-honoring," which was in turn qualified by "Spirit-filled." The logic behind those piled-on modifiers seems to be that the more labels we attach, the greater the margin of theological safety. It is a flawed premise, of course, since we ourselves are the standard by which the measure is taken.

It sounds a bit like the old Quaker who said to his spouse, "Wife, the whole world is queer but me and thee, and sometimes I wonder about thee." If the process continues, one day we might find unacceptable everyone who hasn't been cloned in our own exact image—although, quite frankly, I doubt that I could stand two of me, even if one were a clone.

Edwin Markham wrote four little lines in a poem he called *Outwitted* that have profoundly affected my life:

> He drew a circle that shut me out—
> Heretic, rebel, a thing to flout,
> But Love and I had the wit to win:
> We drew a circle that took him in.[1]

How can we who have received love so indiscriminately justify dispensing it so selectively?

The story is told of a traveler crossing the desert who came at nightfall to a small tent where he asked for food and shelter. "What do you call your god?" the host asked. When the traveler replied that he did not believe in God, the man turned him away.

The Lord appeared to the tent dweller in his troubled sleep and asked about the guest. "I put him out of my tent," the man replied, "because he had no god."

Then the Lord said, "If you will go outside and look up, you will see by the light of the stars of a sky far greater than the roof of your tent. I have not shut anyone out because he didn't know as much as he ought to know. If I can give shelter to the unworthy in my vast world, could you not give your unworthy guest a little shelter in your tiny tent?"

When Jesus told us to love even our enemies, he was trying to teach us that living in love is the only way to be liberated from hate. It was a new principle of the Kingdom, the new society he came to establish.

A few years ago I was leading a conference in Latin America that was attended by church leaders from across the continent. They represented every political coloration and theological category. There were Catholics and evangelicals, Sandinista sympathizers from Nicaragua and supporters of a repressive regime in Chile, doctrinaire conservatives and those who passionately promoted liberation theology. And as you would expect, there were those who wanted violent revolution and others who wanted to preserve the status quo.

Sharp lines of division ran through the conference in every direction. On the first day, the atmosphere was colder than an Arctic night. There were sharp words and cutting innuendos. As the hours dragged by I had begun to wish I was not their chairman.

That night I asked God for help to achieve some kind of breakthrough in relationships. I knew it was futile to hope for agreement. As far as I was concerned, that wasn't even desirable. Our beliefs were sincere and deeply held, and a reconciliation of beliefs wasn't necessary for us to have love and respect for each other as human beings.

The next morning I went to the flip chart and put a series of isolated dots on a clean sheet. Around each dot I drew a small circle. This was the way I felt about yesterday, I said. Each of us was a dot with a tight little circle drawn around him- or herself, excluding everyone else. Then I went went on to explain that I myself do that when I feel afraid and threatened. When that happens, I protect myself with isolation.

"But I want to show you my circle today," I told them, as I drew a sweeping embrace around the whole sheet while quoting Edwin Markham's little poem. "I may not be in your circle," I said, "but you are in mine, and there is nothing you can do to get out. You can't resign, walk out, or run away. If you try it, I will just draw a bigger circle."

And then I asked, "Isn't this what Jesus has done for each of us? Can we—dare we—do less for each other? Love doesn't require you to endorse anybody else's theology or politics. But I wonder . . . in the way we feel about each other as persons, can today be different from yesterday?" Slowly, the tension eased as we accepted being together inside God's big circle.

When I lapse back into my old behavior and start drawing small circles it is because I'm afraid of the dragons and monsters beyond the parameters I have established. When Jesus reached outside the conventional boundaries, he discovered those dragons and monsters to be nothing more than ordinary people who were in desperate need of love. They only appeared scary because of their disguises—tax collectors, disfigured lepers, prostitutes, half-breed Samaritans, revolutionary zealots, rich young rulers, and Roman army officers.

These were the labels stuck on them by other people. Inside, they were just regular folks—frightened and lonely and heartsick, hungering for somebody to take the risk of reaching out to touch them. Jesus took the risk and changed the boundary markings forever.

But let us go further.

To love beyond the boundaries means to love prodigally, not miserly. The word *prodigal* means "waster." That's what the prodigal son was—a waster. He wasted his father's wealth on temporary fun. He wasted his early years in meaningless living. He wasted his virility on prostitutes.

Prodigal love may sound like a strange and stretched dimension. But loving prodigally is different from living prodigally. Life is to be cherished and savored, treated as a sacred stewardship. Love is to be scattered with freedom and outrageous joy. It is a renewable resource that doesn't have to be rationed. Love can be given away without measuring, knowing that none of it will be wasted.

The Cross is the greatest act of prodigal love the world has ever seen.

Do you remember the story of the woman who lavished an entire vial of expensive perfume on the head of Jesus just before his crucifixion? It was a prodigal act, a shameful waste of money in the eyes of the practical, penny-pinching disciples. They scolded her for the waste, but Jesus praised her love and affirmed her gift. To him, it was a marvelous act of spontaneous love that was not to be subject to a cost/benefit analysis.

Why can't we have more spontaneity in love? If we loved more often on impulse, we would also love more prodigally. Wouldn't that be glorious! If you take time to look at love's price tag, probably you've already decided that you aren't prepared to pay whatever love's action will require. Prodigal love doesn't care about cost, because it is irrational anyhow, given in joyous abandon. When is the last time you have given or received love like that? I hope it was recent enough for you to remember how uncommonly wonderful it felt.

But we are so hung up on doing everything right that we often neglect to show love even when we feel like it. We are afraid we'll do it wrong. When I was in high school, one of the sophomore basketball players went to our coach and asked how he should approach a particular girl to ask her for a date. The coach said, "Son, there aren't any wrong ways."

It's that way about acts of love. No loving action can be done in a wrong way. The love motive always redeems it. Leo Buscaglia, a psychologist who teaches and writes about love, says, "The loving person has no need to be perfect, only human."

The kind of love Jesus is talking about in the Sermon on the Mount—love that indiscriminately embraces the world—has an ineffable healing and redemptive quality in it.

During the Vietnam war, World Vision, of which I was then president, started a halfway house in Saigon where orphaned and abandoned babies could be brought for medical treatment before going on to a regular orphanage. With a capacity for seventy-five babies, it was often full as these little pieces of driftwood from a fractured society were picked up out of doorways and off garbage dumps and brought to the facility.

On my first visit to the recovery center, I was being shown around by Dr. Wayne McKinney, whose vision had made it possible. In the first room, I saw babies who had just been brought in. They were malnourished and sick, with arms and legs like matchsticks and faces that looked old. But something puzzled me. In crib after crib, I saw these small bundles drawn up in what seemed to be the fetal position.

When I inquired what this meant Wayne told me it was a syndrome called anaclitic depression. Deep inside their psyches, these babies sensed their rejection by a society brutalized by twenty-five years of conflict that had no place for the unwanted. The fetal position was their subconscious cry to go back to their mother's womb, where they had been warm and nourished, secure and accepted.

Then Dr. McKinney guided me into the next room. It was large and airy, filled with the beautiful, soft music of woodwinds and strings. As I looked around, I saw Vietnamese nurses holding babies and gently rocking them as they stroked them and talked or sang to them. Other babies were in their cribs, sleeping soundly, their little bodies filled out, arms and legs relaxed.

The doctor explained that these babies had been there for several weeks. Medicine and food had healed their bodies, but the lavish love of those nurses prodigally given, the touch of their hands and the gentle sound of their voices, had healed the deeper wounds of rejection.

I believe God wants us to live the way those Vietnamese nurses were loving those babies. There are people in our particular worlds who desperately need that kind of live. Our calling as Christians is to give it. Whatever the cost, the reward will be infinitely greater.

Now that we are already far off the map, will you take the risk and go just a little further with me? Loving beyond the boundaries means loving dangerously, not protectively.

It is risky to love with abandon and without counting the cost. It leaves us open to betrayal and hurt. But the only alternative I know is not to love at all, and who could be happy in the cold sterility of a loveless existence? Not I. I'm too warm-blooded for that.

Before Jesus waltzed us past the boundaries by telling us to love enemies as well as neighbors, love was a reciprocal relationship. We loved those who would love us back, just like the scoundrels and pagans did. But that sounds more like a cozy business arrangement than love.

Agape love, which is the divine love Jesus talks about, takes a chance. The psychologist Erich Fromm said once, "Love means to commit oneself without guarantee . . . love is an act of faith, and whoever is of little faith is also of little love."

I am reminded of the risk taken by the bishop in Victor Hugo's *Les Miserables*. He befriended the ex-convict Jean Valjean, who repaid his benefactor by stealing the silver. Valjean was caught by the police and taken back to the bishop's house. Believing there was some hope for the thief, the bishop told the police the silver had been a gift. He then turned to Valjean and said, "I gave you the candlesticks also. Why didn't you take them along with your plates?"

Through this act of vulnerable love, the ex-convict was changed into a decent, caring, and loving person who personified these qualities at great personal hazard throughout the French Revolution. But it is important to remember that the bishop's leap in the dark came with no money-back guarantee. It could have cost him his candlesticks —along with the rest of his silver!

If we are going to take that gamble, we'd better be prepared to lose in the short term. The principle couldn't be better expressed than in the title of a book by Shirley Dykes Kelley, who warns, *Love Is Not for Cowards*.

There is no greater example outside the Bible of the risky nature of agape love than in Dostoevski's *Crime and Punishment*. In this

Russian novel, a young student, Raskolnikov, murders two people for their money. He rationalizes his crime by telling himself, first, that Napoleon killed thousands and became a hero; second, that his victims were unimportant people; and third, that he would use the money to further his career for the good of humanity.

Most of the story, however, is taken up not with the crime but with Raskolnikov's punishment. At first, it is all inside himself. Another person confesses to the crime, so the police are no longer looking for the murderer. Theoretically, Raskolnikov should feel good, but he feels terrible. His guilt rages inside him, and his body, mind, and spirit grind away at each other and wear him down.

Two other characters enter the story. One is the detective Petrovich, who doesn't believe the false confession and continues to search for the murderer. The other is Sonia, a young girl who loves Raskolnikov.

Hers is a rare kind of love. It is definitely not cheap sentiment. First of all, her love drives Raskolnikov to confess that he is the murderer. She tells him he must do penance to try and expiate his guilt. He does. He kisses the ground he has stained with human blood and cries out his confession to the four corners of the earth.

The unusual love of this woman exposes Raskolnikov, forcing the murderer to face himself in order to find healing for his troubled soul. Tough love doesn't avoid reality. Next, Raskolnikov is convicted and sent off to Siberia, suffering from tuberculosis and pneumonia.

It seems that Sonia wins; she has exposed a murderer. Petrovich wins; his sense of justice has been satisfied. Raskolnikov appears to be the only loser.

You may ask, "What kind of love is it when everybody wins but me? What kind of love would cause another to suffer? Love is supposed to protect and conceal, isn't it? What is this love that exposes? If that's love, you can keep it. Maybe hate isn't so fantastic either, but I don't want any part of that kind of love."

Fair questions. Reasonable conclusion.

But the story doesn't end there. Sonia has risked everything, and now she follows Raskolnikov over the hard miles to Siberia. Throughout his long nine-year sentence, she stays by his side. During that interminable time, she keeps herself and her beloved one alive by scrounging whatever food she can find. Her love never quits.

That's real love . . . love beyond the boundaries. It is the love of First Corinthians 13, which believes all things, hopes all things, endures all things. It's the kind of love that stakes everything on what is right and then believes God's justice is tempered with grace and mercy.

In the climactic scene of Dostoevski's story, Raskolnikov receives forgiveness and has a resurrection to new life.

Is it worth the risk to love beyond the boundaries where dragons and sea monsters dwell? I think so. Because of Sonia's agape love, surely a pure type of Calvary love, everybody has won. Perhaps that is the greatest evidence of all that on the strait and narrow there is new life that abounds with freedom and joy.

And that is something to dance about.

4. Outrageous Forgiveness

Except for a brief, two-verse commentary, the Lord's Prayer stands starkly alone in the Sermon on the Mount. In spite of its application as the prayer pattern for all times and in all places, Jesus offers no explanation or illumination, with but one small exception. Others have written thousands of volumes to enhance our understanding of the model prayer. Jesus himself leaves virtually untouched the sixty-six original words he gave in response to the request of his disciples, "Teach us to pray."

The ten words he lifts out for further comment are catapulted forcefully into our minds simply because he chooses them for emphasis. For one thing, this is the only part of the prayer that seems to have a condition attached. Everything else—the praise, petitions, adoration, worship—is quite straightforward.

The fifth petition in the Lord's Prayer is the one Jesus chooses to highlight: "And forgive us our debts, as we forgive our debtors" (Matt. 6:12, KJV). Then, after concluding the prayer, he seems to pause as if to say, "Oh, one thing more." Then he picks it up, "For if you forgive men their trespasses, your heavenly Father also will forgive you; but if you do not forgive men their trespasses, neither will your Father forgive your trespasses" (Matt. 6:14–15).

This special attention by Jesus provides the clue that on the strait and narrow, forgiveness is a big principle; it is not just a pious platitude or a nice maxim. But it is virtually without meaning unless we are willing to go beyond the vague concept of forgiveness as a noun. We've got to move to the transitive verb phase, in which forgiving becomes an action. In other words, the belief must be transcended by the act.

"Everyone says forgiveness is a lovely idea," C. S. Lewis reminds us, "until they have something to forgive." There's the rub. Jesus simply will not let us get away with an intellectual affirmation of an abstract idea. He insists that we cut right to the heart of our pride and ego by practicing what we say we believe. And he insists that we forgive real trespasses against us—all of them—not just imagined ones or a few petty ones carefully selected to keep our ego intact.

Now, I don't know about you, but that goes straight against my natural grain. I do not want to abandon my grievances; my preference is to nurture them. If I can't hold a trespass to trot out now and again to prove how wrong you are, I have cut the ground out from under my private fantasy that I am always right, and that damages my ego. But my pride would suffer an even greater blow if my friends discovered (gasp!) that my image as Mr. Right is often phony.

Do you know the three most satisfying words in the English language you can say to another person? If you guessed, "I love you," you're wrong. Sure, those are nice words—all warm and fuzzy. But if you really want to make somebody's day, simply say, "You are right." That's an ego massage so pleasant that just to contemplate it gives me goose pimples.

Most of us have a human, worldly, consuming urge to be right. It is illustrated by a story I heard of a minister who left his pulpit to go to medical school and become a doctor. An old friend saw him several years later and expressed surprise at his career change, but remarked that he assumed it had been for compassionate reasons.

"Not at all," the doctor responded, "the reasons were purely economic. I discovered that people will pay more money to care for their bodies than for their souls."

Several years lapsed before the friend saw him again and discovered that he had left medicine for law. "What was your reason this time?" the friend asked.

"Simple economics again," replied the ex-minister, ex-doctor attorney. "I discovered that people will pay more to prove they are right than to care for either body or soul."

Could that be why we are such a litigious society? Perhaps the explosion in the number of civil lawsuits has more to do with salvaging ego and pride than with redressing actual wrongs.

If the three sweetest words ever to fall on human ear are "You are right," then surely the three hardest words for any of us to say are "I am wrong." Adam couldn't say them. When God called him to account for having eaten of the tree of the knowledge of good and evil against orders, Adam was unable to take personal responsibility for his actions. He looked around for someone to blame and loaded the guilt on the only two he saw, his wife and God. His disobedience, he insisted, was the fault of "the *woman you* gave me" (italics mine). In other words, she did it to me, but, you, God, are ultimately responsible because you gave her to me when I hadn't even asked for her! Like most of the rest of us, Adam had to be right, even if that meant making God wrong.

I enjoy the comic strip Andy Capp, whose principal character is a chronically unemployed cockney who spends most of his days playing soccer and most of his nights at the corner pub, both of which drive his long-suffering wife, Flo, up the wall. In one episode, Andy is pacing the floor while Flo stands with her arms crossed.

Finally, she breaks the silence: "Three whole days without speaking. This is ridiculous." In the next frame she says to Andy, "I'm sorry I acted the way I did . . . you were right. Friends?"

A bit nonplussed, Andy says, "OK, friends."

Flo hugs him and gives him a kiss on the cheek. As Andy leaves the house, he meets one of his soccer buddies, who says, "I 'eard that, Andy. It takes a good woman to apologize when she is in the wrong."

As they walk down the street, Andy reflects on Chalkie's remark and replies, "It takes a better one to apologize when she's not."

Flo seems to have grasped a significant truth. Maintaining a relationship is much more important than establishing who is right and who is wrong. So often we allow the hurt to deepen because our pride won't let us forgive and forget without having to fix blame.

Several years ago two very fine people on my staff found themselves at loggerheads over a rather trivial matter. Primarily, it had to do with position and wounded pride. Each would talk to me about the other, trying to establish a position of right. The relationship deteriorated, and the atmosphere in the office grew frigid. "Right" and "wrong" became the paramount issue as the original conflict faded into the background. I asked them to work it out between them, since they were both mature people, but pride made it impossible for either of them to initiate a dialogue.

Finally, one day I realized that I probably had the capacity to resolve the whole matter with one stroke. I sat down with them and said something like this: "In rethinking this whole episode, I see something I have not seen before. I am the one who is responsible for the misunderstanding. I failed to communicate clearly to each of you. Your actions were consistent with what you heard. I am the one who was wrong, and the tension between you is my fault. I ask your understanding and forgiveness."

Immediately, both of them relaxed, smiled at me, and then at each other. The issue was settled. I didn't feel that I had lost anything by taking responsibility. Instead, I had gained the loyalty of two fine people and had helped restore harmony between them. And I had learned an important lesson. Flo was right. Maintaining a relationship is better than fixing blame.

Now let's take a close look at the two-verse commentary that Jesus gives us on the fifth petition of the model prayer, "For if you forgive men their trespasses your heavenly Father also will forgive you; but if you do not forgive men their trespasses, neither will your Father forgive your trespasses" (Matt. 6:14–15).

The apparent connection between forgiving others and receiving God's forgiveness is strange. On the surface, it seems to make God's forgiveness conditional. It appears to offer bargaining ground with God. On deeper reflection, however, this appears to be one of those places where Jesus seems to say, "You figure it out."

So let's have a go at it.

First, I am sure that forgiving others is not a meritorious act on our part that earns God's pardon for us. Forgiveness is not a *quid pro quo* arrangement. We have no merit that allows us to demand reciprocity; "In my hand no price I bring, simply to thy cross I cling." The atoning act of the death of Jesus Christ alone commends us to God's grace. For Christ's sake, we have received fully of God's tender mercies, and his free gift is in no way proportionate to any performance on our part.

Second, I am sure that our forgiving behavior is not a pattern for God to use in pardoning offenders. He doesn't need my example, since even my best spiritual performances are flawed and imperfect. In the Old Testament, God pledges to "abundantly pardon" all who seek him, call upon him, give up their wicked ways and unrighteous thoughts, and return to him (Isa. 55:6–7). Pardoning and forgiving are his divine prerogatives, and he does not need to be instructed by mortals in those areas where he excels.

If you were head of the divine personnel department charged with drafting a job description for God, pardoning and forgiving would be right at the top of the list. He does those things with such flair. The prophet Isaiah continues, with God connecting this activity with his Godship, "For my thoughts are not your thoughts, neither are your ways my ways . . . so are my ways higher than your ways and my thoughts than your thoughts" (55:8–9). There is nothing reasonable or rational about God's forgiveness. It is outrageously illogical.

Third, I am sure that God is not establishing an order of priority for our actions, implying that our forgiving must come before his own. In all acts of love, God is first: "We love him because he first loved us" (1 John 4:19, KJV). His mercy to us is the reason for our mercy to others. Paul establishes the order: "Be kind to one another, tenderhearted, forgiving one another, as God in Christ forgave you" (Eph. 4:32).

We are already forgiven, Paul says, and the natural consequence should be loving behavior toward others. But if there is no transactional theology implied in Jesus' short commentary on the fifth petition, there are a couple of ways in which forgiving and being forgiven are connected. For one thing, if we indulge ourselves in rigid, unbending, and vindictive behavior along with maintaining a bitter, resentful, and obstinate attitude, then we have no capacity to receive God's mercy. It would be like trying to pour a glass of clean water into a glass already filled with dirty water. The glass must be emptied before it can be filled.

Or, it would be like opening the gates of an irrigation canal only to discover that no water can reach the parched fields because of a clogged channel. The debris in the channel must be cleared away first, so God's abundant pardon can flow into us. There are not two parallel channels marked In and Out or Receiving and Giving. One through-channel serves both functions.

That is what Jesus had in mind, I believe, when he linked God's forgiveness with our practice of forgiving others. It is a big principle. The reason forgiveness is up there at the top is that it is the one unique, exclusive, and stellar commodity the Church can offer the world.

It isn't ethics or judgment or morals. Robert Capon explains it this way: "The church is not in the morals business. The world is in the morals business, quite rightfully; and it has done a fine job of it, all things considered.... What the world cannot get right, however, is the forgiveness business—and that, of course, is the church's real job.... She is not in the business of telling the world what's right and wrong so that it can do good and avoid evil. She is in the business of offering, to a world which knows all about that tiresome subject, forgiveness for its chronic unwillingness to take its own advice."[1]

Jesus told us in the story of the prodigal son that forgiveness and acceptance are reasons for throwing a party and dancing. Forgiveness, especially of the outrageous, irrational kind, is just that sort of liberating experience.

For one thing, when I forgive, I release myself. One morning Nancy came back from walking our little Pekingese and made an announcement. "I have just discovered something. I am on the other end of Mtoki's leash! But I still haven't figured out whether he's the one who's hooked, or if I am."

I haven't figured that one out either, but I know that when I am leashed to another person by resentment and hatred, I am the one who is hooked. It is my physic energy I am burning up, my sleep that is being disturbed, my stomach that is pumping the acid, my colitis that flares up, my body that feels the stress and inner pain. Often the other person doesn't even know the bitterness I feel, so I am the sole sufferer in a sick relationship.

With perceptive insight, the author Lewis Smedes calls our attention to Michael Christopher's play *The Black Angel*. It is about a Nazi general, Herman Engel, who was sentenced to thirty years in prison for atrocities committed during the war by his troops. Released at the end of his term, he and his wife retired to Alsace, where they built a cabin in the woods and hoped to live out their years in anonymity and peace.

But a French journalist, Morrieaux, had other plans for the former Nazi. Engel's army had massacred Morrieaux's entire family, and the journalist had personally sentenced Engel to death even if the Nuremberg court had given him only thirty years.

When Engel was released, Morrieaux shadowed him, nurturing his feelings of hate until the right moment. Finally, he was able to stir up the fanatics in the nearby village, they made plans on a certain night to go up the hill to torch Engel's cabin and shoot the former Nazi commander and his wife.

But Morrieaux had some unfinished business with Engel, so he went up the hill in the afternoon to confront Engel and fill in the gaps in his story. Engel was shaken to be recognized, but Morrieaux was even more disturbed because the ex-general looked less like the monster he hated than he did an ordinary, tired old man. Besides, the writer couldn't put the pieces of the village massacre together as neatly as he had thought, so his concentrated, industrial-strength hatred was being diluted, and he became more and more confused.

Before the afternoon was over, Morrieaux told Engel the villagers were coming that night to kill him. He offered to lead his enemy out of the woods and save his life. By now, Engel himself was possessed by doubts of his own, and he made this strange statement, "I'll go with you on one condition."

Imagine! A man who is going to die within a few hours sets conditions for his rescue! He must be mad! But Engel tells Morrieaux his condition for going with him: "That you forgive me."

That is something Morrieaux cannot do. For over thirty years he has honed his hatred to a razor-sharp edge. Give up his obsession? It had been a part of his every waking moment. He could not live without his hate. His hatred didn't belong to him; he belonged to it. Having harbored it for so long, he had made his hate part of his identity.

He would thwart the execution, but forgive Engel? Never! That night, the villagers came and murderously ended Morrieaux's 30-year-old nightmare. Engel and his wife were killed, their cottage burned. But there is no evidence that Morrieaux felt any better for the vengeance he had perpetrated.

Dr. Smedes concludes the story, "The tragedy was that only forgiveness, the one thing he could not give to Engel, could have set Morrieaux free."[2]

Morrieaux seems not to have understood that when we forgive someone, we liberate ourselves.

Not only that, but in the act of forgiving someone, we also release the other person. We give up our power over that person without needing to make him or her suffer in some way. That is redemptive forgiveness. On the cross at Golgotha, Jesus showed us how to forgive that way. No words spoken by Jesus are as self-authenticating as his prayer from the cross, "Father, forgive them; for they know not what they do" (Luke 23:34).

Someone has said that those words are a Jesus original. No one had ever before breathed that prayer, certainly not from a cross.

When Mahatma Gandhi was assassinated, he instinctively threw up his hand in the Hindu gesture of forgiveness. Gandhi understood what Jesus was about, or else he never could have said, "The weak can never forgive. Forgiveness is an attribute of the strong." His whole nonviolent struggle for justice was an acknowledgment of a debt to the Teacher of forgiveness.

When the German Lutheran pastor Martin Niemöller was in the concentration camp at Dachau as a political prisoner, the gallows stood outside his window. He saw thousands of prisoners go to their deaths. Some cursed, some whimpered, some prayed.

Pastor Niemöller asked himself this: "What will happen on the day they lead you there and put you to the test? When they put that rope around your neck, what will be your last words? Will you then cry out, 'You criminals, scum! There's a God in heaven! You'll get yours!'

"What if Jesus had said that, if he had taken his last breath to cry out to the soldiers and the Sanhedrin, 'Criminals! Scum! This is my Father's world. You'll get yours!'?

"What would have happened? Nothing! One more poor sinner would have died there, lonely and forgotten, and nothing would have happened."

If Jesus had sought vengeance, called his enemies to account, cursed his executioners, pleaded his rights, or demanded justice, no one would have been surprised, and he would have died as just one more sorry spectacle of broken, flawed, self-centered humanity. His name would not have been remembered beyond his generation. God's redemptive plan rested not simply on the character of Jesus' life but on the quality of his death.

The forgiveness prayer from the cross was Jesus' way of releasing those who were hooked by their own hatred. God has a most unusual strategy for winning over his enemies. It scarcely seems like a power play at all, certainly not one designed to defeat his enemies. He is winning by losing, saving by loving, living by dying, and fighting by forgiving. Admittedly, that's a strange formula for anybody but God.

"It took me a long time to learn," Pastor Niemöller said, "that God is not the enemy of my enemies. God is not even the enemy of his enemies!"

One of President Abraham Lincoln's associates scolded him rather severely for being soft on his enemies. "Why do you insist on trying to make friends of them?" he chided. "You should be trying to destroy them."

To which Lincoln replied gently, "Am I not destroying my enemies when I make them my friends?" In speaking of those who were his enemies during the Civil War, Lincoln is reported to have said, "Insane as it may seem, I hold malice toward none of them. I have neither the time nor the energy in this life to hold that kind of resentment."

When we forgive, we have chosen to resolve our own hurt by love rather than by settling the score. That is the way God does it, and that is what he asks us to do. That is the way Jesus practiced forgiveness on the cross.

And that is an outrageously uncommon attitude.

Finally, when we choose to live a forgiving life, we release God's power in us. It is like the alabaster box of ointment the woman broke in order to release its perfume on Jesus. Until our pride and ego are broken in the practice of forgiveness, the treasure remains locked away inside us, and we never experience its redemptive power.

One day when I was walking along a trail in East Africa with some friends, I became aware of a delightful odor that filled the air. I looked up in the trees and around at the bushes in an effort to discover where it was coming from. Then my friends told me to look down at the small blue flower growing on along the path. Each time we crushed the tiny blossoms under our feet, more of its sweet perfume was released into the air. Then my friends said, "We call it the forgiveness flower."

I understood what they meant, and I prayed to be like that flower. It didn't wait until we asked forgiveness for crushing it. It did not release its fragrance in measured doses or hold us to a reciprocal arrangement. It didn't ask for an apology; it merely lived up to its name and forgave—freely, fully, richly. What a touching example of outrageous forgiveness!

A German novelist of the last century, Jean Paul Richter, expressed the idea this way: "Humanity is never so beautiful as when praying for forgiveness, or else forgiving another."

I can't read that comment without thinking of John Perkins, a man I admire very much. Both John and I were born in Mississippi but a couple of years and a world apart. We were both poor, growing up during the Great Depression, but John was black and I was white. In those days, few people even thought about trying to bridge the chasm.

My family moved west long before the civil rights movement came to Mississippi. John went west, too, but he chose to return home in the early 1970s to push for civil rights for his people. That took a lot of courage, because it was a dangerous time to champion the rights of blacks in the South.

John led a boycott against white merchants in the town of Mendenhall, and from that moment on he was a marked man. One Saturday night he and a group of college students en route to Jackson were arrested on trumped-up charges in the town of Brandon. The beatings started even before they got to the jail. But once inside the "security" of the jail the leaders of the group were selected for special attention.

John tells what it was like: "During the beatings, I tried to cover my head with my arms, but they just beat me anyway till I was lying on the floor. Even then they just kept on beating and stomping me, kicking me in the head, in the ribs, in the groin. . . . Because I was unconscious a lot of the time, I don't remember a whole lot except that there was blood all over. And a lot of it was mine."

When a rumor circulated that the FBI was on the way, the police ordered John to mop up the blood on the floor. "I did my best," John recalls, "but I was so weak and wobbly and in so much pain. Blood was still pouring from my head, and it didn't help a whole lot that some of the police kept on beating me while I tried to mop up my own blood."

The FBI never came, and the beatings got worse as the night wore on: "They were like savages—like some horror out of the night. And I can't forget their faces, so twisted with hate. It was like looking at white-faced demons. Hate did that to them.

"But you know, I couldn't hate back. When I saw what hate had done to them, I couldn't hate back. I could only pity them. I didn't ever want hate to do to me what it had already done to those men. . . . The Spirit of God kept working on me and in me until I could say with Jesus, 'I forgive them, too.'"[3]

Difficult as it is, such outrageous forgiveness is not beyond the reach of any of us. Jesus gave dramatic evidence of that at Calvary. But it cannot be done by willpower or in the energy of the flesh. When we pray to forgive our debtors, we are asking for a miracle. We are handed some deals that are so raw that the mind cannot simply dismiss them. We discover that the grace of forgiveness lies beyond our human ability. That is why we must ask God for the power to forgive.

That was the experience of Corrie ten Boom. During World War II, this Dutch woman and her sister, Betsie, were put in the concentration camp at Ravensbruck because her family hid Jews during the Nazi occupation. Betsie died, but Corrie survived, and after the war, she told her story as a Christian all over the world. She was afraid that some day she would meet one of her jailers, and she wondered what she would do.

It happened at a church service in Munich. A former SS officer who had stood guard at the door of the women's shower was there. Corrie was flooded with repugnant memories. After the meeting, he came up beaming and bowing. "How grateful I am for your message, Fraulein," he said. "To think that, as you say, he has washed my sins away!"

He then thrust out his hand to Corrie. "And I," Corrie says, "who had preached so often . . . the need to forgive, kept my hand at my side."

She was ashamed and convicted by her angry, vengeful thoughts. "Lord Jesus, forgive me, and help me to forgive him," she prayed. Nothing happened. She felt no warmth or charity, nor could she raise her hand. Again she breathed a silent prayer: "Jesus, I cannot forgive him; give me your forgiveness."

Corrie describes what happened next: "As I took his hand the most incredible thing happened. From my shoulder along my arm and through my hand a current seemed to pass from me to him, while into my heart sprang a love for this stranger that almost overwhelmed me."[4]

According to the Swiss theologian Johann Lavater, "He who has not forgiven an enemy has never yet tasted one of the most sublime enjoyments of life." My friend John Perkins has known such a sublime moment. So did Corrie ten Boom.

Is it possible to forgive and forget? Some think not. Others think it is an irrelevant question. Still others think we should not forget, that forgiveness is even more divine when the gravity of the wrong is remembered. Personally, I do not know for sure. But I have come to believe that it is possible to forget the injustice to the point where it no longer makes any difference, and that is what really counts.

Unfortunately, too many of us put the hurt into our memory bank so it can be called up in case we need it in a vengeful moment. That hardly seems to be the outrageous dimension of forgiveness Jesus is talking about in the Lord's Prayer.

In his fantasy story *Through the Looking Glass*, Lewis Carroll sets up this enlightening exchange between the king and queen:

> "The horror of that moment," the King said,
> I shall never, never forget."
> "You will though," said the Queen, "If you
> don't make a memorandum of it."

Perhaps that is the secret of forgetting, not to make a memo of the wrong. Charles Simmons, an eighteenth-century clergyman and author, said, "There is a noble forgetfulness—that which does not remember injuries."

Less negative and even more profound, however, is an insight by James Hilton, who wrote *Goodbye, Mr. Chips* and *Lost Horizon*. Just before he died in 1954, Hilton said, "If you forgive people enough you belong to them, and they to you, whether either person likes it or not—squatter's rights of the heart."

That is outrageous forgiveness, and I, for one, find it a troubling thought. Yet I dare not reject it, for it is through such risky forgiveness, fully received and freely given, that God liberates us for the dance.

5. Getting Even Is a High-Ticket Item

When I take our dog out for a walk, our usual route takes us along a street on which a small sports car is parked. It is one of those with a Z or *ST* or some other letters combined with a set of numbers that are supposed to give it power before you ever give it the gas. Sleek and low-slung, shiny and sparkling, the vehicle serves as much to make a statement about the owner as it does for transportation, I sometimes suspect.

One morning I noticed a sticker mounted on the dashboard. Without any attempt at subtlety, it said, "I don't get mad; I get even." I got to thinking about that as the dog and I continued our walk. It put a chill on an otherwise beautiful morning. So much of our society seems to be ordered by the law of payback instead of the grace of forgiveness.

I remembered Jesus' advice about revenge in the Sermon on the Mount. Following his pattern of contrasting the new order with the old traditions, he said, "You have heard that it was said, 'An eye for an eye, and a tooth for a tooth.' But I say to you, do not resist him who is evil; but whoever slaps you on your right cheek, turn to him the other also. And if any one wants to sue you, and take your shirt, let him have your coat also. And whoever shall force you to go one mile, go with him two. Give to him who asks of you, and do not turn away from him who wants to borrow from you" (Matt. 5:38–42, NASB).

It's a grand concept for a world in which there are perfect people. Too bad, though, that the world is imperfect and Jesus is so impractical. If he understood the dog-eat-dog world we live in today, he would know that kind of passive piety never works. This is the twentieth century, and our Golden Rule is, "Do it unto others before they do it unto you." We flaunt bumper stickers that read, "Two wrongs don't make it right, but it makes it even."

We are a "get even" society, by legal means if possible or violent ones if it isn't. We tend to think that only a Goody Two-Shoes or a Pollyanna really believes that the noble idealism in the Sermon on the Mount has any practical application to daily life in our complex and turbulent world.

Since most of us are hard-headed, tough-as-shoe-leather realists, what are we to make of this teaching about the other cheek, the surrendered coat, the second mile, the spontaneous loan? For a moment, forget these applications that Jesus mentions. Later on you can make a list of specifics that fit your own life.

For now, let's explore the principle on which Jesus bases his applications. Certainly he is not negating the principle of self-preservation by telling us that we should become the floor mats of a society that is innately hostile to Kingdom people. It is true, though, that some people act as if they truly believe that the more passive they are, the more they display Christian virtue. So they go through life with a beatific smile pasted on their faces, revealing no feelings. But there isn't any virtue, Christian or otherwise, in being a Caspar Milquetoast.

However, I've come to question whether there are any truly passive persons in the world. Instead, in my experience the ones who appear to be docile and unperturbed turn out to be what psychologists call passive-aggressive. And as a rule, they are intensely hostile below the surface.

I don't believe that Jesus ever affirmed either by his life or by his teachings that nonassertiveness is to be equated with spirituality.

Rather, I believe that in these verses Jesus is giving us the great principle of forbearance, gentleness, and long-suffering, and is forbidding a spirit of revenge over any perceived personal wrongs. He is saying in effect, "On the strait and narrow, you are free from having your behavior determined by the way you are treated. When you are mistreated, you don't have to respond with a kneejerk reaction. You can choose your response instead of obeying your egocentric impulses. You are liberated to live by the law of love. You may get angry, but you don't have to get even."

This is no little platitude, and it shouldn't be tossed aside merely because it seems impractical in today's boisterous world. We shouldn't try to find the meaning in the "letter" of the teaching, but in its "spirit." Whenever we are gentle, long-suffering, patient with others, willing to bear personal insult or injury, unwilling to strike back, large-hearted and kind-handed, we are on the strait and narrow and are acting like Kingdom people.

Now, the kind of behavior Jesus is suggesting isn't easy, because it cuts against the grain of basic human nature. The oldest law of behavior in the world is stated in these words: "An eye for an eye and a tooth for a tooth." The first appearance of this rule was in Hammurabi's Code far back in history and it was included in the Mosaic laws as well. But it is important for us to understand that its inclusion in the Old Testament was not a command to retribution but a limitation on vengeance. No penalty could be greater than the extent of the crime. The law of payback and revenge is embedded in many primitive cultures and not a few modern ones as well. In fact, but for the grace of God it is a virus that infects us all. And what a high price we pay for the luxury of hating and plotting revenge!

Dale Carnegie tells of a visit to Yellowstone Park in earlier days when tourists could watch the rangers feed the grizzly bears. One night the ranger brought garbage to attract the huge creatures, who, it is said, can whip any animal in the West except perhaps the buffalo and the Kodiak bear. But Carnegie noticed that the bears would allow one little animal to eat with them. The others were sent scurrying with growls—all except the skunk! Though it was obvious that the grizzlies resented the skunk for its brazen impudence and would have loved to have their revenge, they didn't. And, you can guess why. The cost of getting even was just too high![1]

Smart grizzly! Smarter than a lot of us humans who spend frustrating days and sleepless nights brooding over resentments and plotting ways to get even. Those feelings of resentment, bitterness, and revenge exact a heavy toll in your body, soul, and emotions. It is even possible to harbor these feelings for so long that we can't live without them. But the cost is outrageously high and damaging.

By the time the longest and most savage of America's inter-family feuds ended in the late 1800s, its origins already had become obscure. Nobody knew for sure how it had begun. One historian has said that the bitter disputes that arose between mountaineers were mostly over trifling matters, such as livestock, women, politics, and thievery. I can't believe that he included politics and women as "trifling matters." The man obviously knew more about history than he did about life!

Some historians say the fuse for the Hatfield-McCoy powder-keg that exploded on the mountains of Kentucky and West Virginia was lit during the Civil War but kept burning by disputes over a $1.75 fiddle and a stray razorback hog. The fuse reached the powder during election day festivities in 1882 when three McCoy brothers killed Ellison Hatfield because he had insulted them. "Devil Anse," head of the Hatfield clan, had the three McCoys rounded up and tied to bushes within sight of their family cabin; then he put fifty rifle bullets into them. After that it was a life for a life—sometimes two or three—and even the women became just part of the body count.

The feud was mostly over by 1890, although there were flare-ups nearly to the turn of the century, and the hostilities didn't finally abate until the second decade of the twentieth century. But the cost to the two families was immense—nearly half a century of bitterness and almost thirty known deaths. It was a high price tag to put on what we sometimes call "sweet revenge."

A part of the price we pay for the privilege of plotting revenge is the loss of joy and peace of mind. No one can be happy and serene when the roots of an emotional cancer run deep into the soul, spreading deadly toxins that poison the mind and spirit.

A few years ago I was in the jungles of Papua New Guinea visiting a primitive tribe that had never had contact with the outside world until the mid-1970s. For centuries, they had lived in jungle isolation by the law of payback, under which every slight or wrong required retribution, usually a killing. If a man suspected another of stealing from his taro patch, he would hide beside a trail and kill the thief. This in turn required a revenge murder, which prompted further escalation in a never-ending cycle. The tribe had become so fragmented through fear of each other that they were reduced to living in small, isolated family units. Life was constant terror and hardship.

One day they heard from a Christian of another tribe that there was a new way of life – a way, according to the Pidgin English, to live *belesi*. They then asked for a missionary to come and teach them. And when I visited their small community on the banks of the April River, Fritz Urschitz from Austria had been living among them for a couple of years.

Gradually, they were emerging from their darkness, coming into the light, learning to live by the law of gentleness and love instead of the law of payback. They called it living *belesi*. We would call it "peace of mind," but the transliteration from Pidgin is "easy in the belly." Those Nikseks may be primitive in their culture, but they know more than we do about the connection between physical and emotional well-being. In reality the seat of our emotions is not in the heart or in the head, but in the pit of our stomach, where we pay a high price in ill health and physical discomfort for the privilege of hanging onto feelings of bitterness and hostility.

Jesus knew what he was talking about. Getting even is a high-ticket item. It is for our own physical and emotional health that we are admonished to substitute positive actions for negative attitudes. That is the most important aspect of his teaching on revenge in the Sermon on the Mount.

The specific actions that Jesus urges on us are not a demonstration of weakness or a surrender to raw power. On the contrary, turning the other cheek, giving away our outer garment and going further than required are positive responses that reflect our freedom to live by the higher law of love.

The apostle Paul makes his own list of specific actions to illustrate the same principle, "If someone has done you wrong, do not repay him with a wrong. Try to do what everyone considers to be good. Do everything possible on your part to live in peace with everybody. Never take revenge, my friends, but instead let God's anger do it. For the scripture says: 'I will take revenge, I will pay back, says the Lord.' Instead, as the scripture says: 'If your enemy is hungry, feed him; if he is thirsty, give him a drink; for by doing this you will make him burn with shame.' Do not let evil defeat you; instead, conquer evil with good" (Rom. 12:17–21, TEV).

Vengeance is God's territory, and it is disastrous for us to invade it. If we trespass, there is no way to avoid getting hooked by feelings of bitterness and hatred. God is the only one who can even the score redemptively. Both Jesus and Paul tell us that our role in the revenge drama is to act generously toward an enemy. Only in so doing are we able to transcend the idea that vengeance always means punishment.

When we can do that, we are living in the freedom of the Kingdom.

The moment we start plotting revenge, we pay for it with our freedom. We become another person's slave and allow that person to so control our thoughts that we are no longer able to live serenely.

Are we less smart than the grizzlies? Is that why we fill every waking moment with feelings and thoughts that fume like acid and corrode deep inside our emotional center?

The story of Haman from the Book of Esther is a textbook case of what resentment will do to a person. Haman was prime minister of Persia, the number two man in the kingdom. He had everything, including the homage of all the palace functionaries, that is, all but one. Mordecai refused to bow when Haman passed by, because it would have violated his Jewish faith to worship anyone but God.

Haman interpreted this as a snub. It made him furious, and he brooded over it. Without Mordecai, he was sure his life would be perfect. Do you recognize the feeling? So, as the story goes, Haman plotted to get even. He would get his revenge on Mordecai by killing all the Jews in Persia, a classic case of overkill if ever there was one. Through a subterfuge, he even managed to get the king's approval in spite of the fact that the king's favorite consort, Queen Esther, was herself a Jew.

Mordecai heard about the plan and persuaded Esther to appeal to the king. She agreed and invited both the king and Haman to a dinner in her private quarters. Haman was elated, but when he left the palace after enjoying the banquet he saw Mordecai there at the gate and was furious because he refused to bow down when Haman's party went by.

When Haman arrived home and told his wife about his honors and his private invitation to the queen's dinner, he added petulantly, "But none of this means anything to me as long as I see that Jew Mordecai sitting at the entrance of the palace" (Esther 5:13, TEV). Haman had become a slave to the man he hated, allowing his bitterness to poison even what should have been happy moments. His wife then suggested that he build a scaffold and work things out to get the king's permission to hang Mordecai.

Haman did as his wife suggested and got the scaffold ready, and then went to the palace to persuade the king to go along with his plan.

In the meantime, though, the king had just been reading some historical records and remembered that a Jew named Mordecai had once saved him from assassination. When the king checked whether Mordecai had ever been rewarded, he was told that nothing had been done. Later, then, when Haman arrived the king asked him for suggestions on how to honor a man who had pleased him.

Guess who Haman thought the king had in mind? Why, the number two man in the empire! None other than Haman himself. So he proposed lavish treatment for such a man, suggesting that he be dressed in the king's own robe and crown, and put on the king's horse and that one of the noblemen should lead the horse through the streets shouting, "This is the way the king honors those who truly please him!"

The whole scenario came off just as Haman suggested, but the actors were in different roles. Mordecai was on the horse, and Haman was doing the shouting. Haman was thoroughly humiliated, but he recovered enough to get to Queen Esther's second banquet, and that was his second mistake of the day. Between the main course and dessert, Esther told the king about the plot to kill all the Jews, including herself, and named Haman as the instigator.

The king was shocked and ordered Haman's death. Told by one of his aides that a new 75-foot gallows had just been built in Haman's courtyard, the king ordered that Haman be hanged on his own scaffold. When "revenge proves to be its own executioner," as John Ford once put it, getting even is truly a high-ticket item.

If the gate is strait and the way is narrow into God's Kingdom, there is little room for one whose arms are piled high with resentment, bitterness, and hatred. Somewhere they've got to be dealt with and laid down. Held onto, they could cost you the Kingdom. Saying yes to Christ means saying no to other things so we can be true to the yes.

It is likely, at this point, somebody somewhere is jumping up and down to justify a grievance, "You don't know how badly I have been mistreated, how flagrant has been the injustice, how terrible has been the hurt."

That's true. I don't know. But I do know the principle. And I think it is not unfair to ask, "Has your treatment been worse than Joseph's at the hands of his own brothers?" He was sold into slavery in Egypt while still a young man, thought dead by his father, put in a dungeon for rejecting the sexual advances of his employer's wife. He could have been consumed with the desire for revenge.

But Joseph had faith to believe that God would ultimately smooth off all the ragged corners of his life and that he would work for Joseph's good even through mistreatment and injustice. He never got bitter, never allowed hate to take control of his feelings, and never plotted revenge. Leaving vengeance up to God, Joseph allowed God's power to be constantly released in him. He simply played the role assigned to him in the revenge drama: he replaced a negative attitude with a positive action by behaving generously and lovingly toward his enemies.

God's way of getting "vengeance" in the end was to use Joseph to save from famine, not only the whole country of Egypt, but his own brothers and family as well! That's a new twist, isn't it? Could it be that one of the reasons we don't want to leave vengeance to God is that we are afraid he may act like God and do some loving thing instead of acting like us and wreaking appropriate punishment on the culprit?

In his essay "On Revenge," Francis Bacon said, "In taking revenge, a man is but even with his enemy; but in passing it over, he is superior." Isn't this what Jesus did? Everything he taught in the Sermon on the Mount, he demonstrated on the mount of his crucifixion. He showed us how the love principle works. Because Jesus refused to hate and think vengeful thoughts, he was free to choose his response to those who crucified him. He chose to love them and forgive them. And by his actions, he made it plain, "No matter what you do to me, I am free to love you and I will love you."

It was a humid Sunday in the summer of 1974 and Atlanta's Ebenezer Baptist Church was packed. The congregation was singing the Lord's Prayer as Dr. Martin Luther King, Sr., prepared to go to the pulpit. He sat with his head bowed.

At the organ was Alberta, his wife of fifty years. His pet name for her was Honeybunch, shortened most of the time to just Bunch. For half of those fifty years, she had been organist and choir director at Ebenezer. Founded by her father, this church had been the focal point of her life. Her martyred son had grown up in Ebenezer and had served as pastor with his father.

As the worshipers came to the part of the song that said, "Forgive us our debts as we forgive our debtors," Mrs. King played the notes plaintively soft. At this point, a mentally disturbed man jumped up from his seat just a few pews away, pulled out two pistols and shouted obscenities as he started firing wildly.

The first shot hit Mrs. King, and her lifeblood stained the instrument as she slumped over the keyboard. Within seconds, Daddy King had her in his arms, and within minutes she was dead.

The two people who were the dearest on earth to him, his wife and his son, had both been taken from him violently. Now he was seventy-six and virtually alone, but still he could find no room in his heart for bitterness. When asked about the attempt to seek the death penalty for his wife's killer, Daddy King became emotional, "Please don't let them kill him! Oh, please don't let them do that. That won't bring her back. God's been too good to me for me to hate. He's just a boy. God loves him. God can forgive him. I forgive him. I can't hate. God has been too good to me for me to hate."

Leaving revenge in God's hands is a sane, rational, and satisfying decision. Our role—our only role—is to replace our negative attitude with positive actions. On the strait and narrow, we are free from having our behavior determined by the way we are treated. When we are mistreated, we can choose our level of response instead of giving in to our egocentric impulses. Then we are liberated to live by the law of love.

We may get angry, but we don't have to get even. Besides, it is impossible to concentrate on the dance while plotting to even the score.

6. Matching the Inside and the Outside

A few months before Peter Sellers died, *Time* magazine featured the actor in a cover story. Commenting on his versatility, the magazine reported a very revealing story about Sellers's appearance on "The Muppet Show." Evidently Kermit the Frog told him that it was all right to "just relax and be yourself." To which Sellers replied, "I could never be myself. You see, there is no me. I do not exist."

The *Time* article saw this exchange as a good joke, but then went on to comment, "The real Peter Sellers at fifty-four, is virtually a cipher." Apparently, during his entire life, he never discovered the real person beneath the veneer. A long-time friend once said of him, "Peter is the accumulation of all the roles he's played and all the people he's met. He's directing traffic inside all that."[1]

People in the acting profession who live with so much pretense may be especially vulnerable, but they are not the only victims of this cultural syndrome. In our society today, identity and self-worth—those Siamese twins of spiritual health—are so much determined by the public roles we play that few indeed are fortunate enough to be able to cut through the exterior gloss to get to their own personhood.

In fact, we are so much preoccupied with image and public roles that we have developed an entire industry to create public images for corporations and products and to keep them burnished bright. The shorthand name for it is Madison Avenue. It is where fantasyland is created, where glitz and show reign over truth and transparency, where reality is altered or sublimated in the name of "whatever sells."

The Madison Avenue virus has infected the church community as well. Anything that puts us in a state of contradiction, that exalts the persona over the real self, that inhibits our efforts at self-understanding, that keeps us from knowing who we are is not our friend.

For example, the kind of Christian television that produces sanctified superstars is no different from television that is designed only to entertain. Both emphasize the artificial and egotistical, and contribute to a personality cult. Neither enhances self-knowledge and awareness, and both are destructive of personhood.

Whatever else Jesus is telling us in the Sermon on the Mount when he uses the metaphors of the healthy tree and the sick one, the good fruit and the rotten, and the wolf in sheep's clothing, he is certainly saying something about the the quality of the inner life:

"Beware of false prophets, who come to you in sheep's clothing but inwardly are ravenous wolves. . . .So, every sound tree bears good fruit, but the bad tree bears evil fruit. A sound tree cannot bear evil fruit, nor can a bad tree bear good fruit. Every tree that does not bear good fruit is cut down and thrown into the fire. . . . On that day many will say to me, 'Lord, Lord, did we not prophesy in your name, and cast out demons in your name, and do many mighty works in your name?' And then will I declare to them, 'I never knew you; depart from me, you evildoers'" (Matt. 7:15–23).

There are three metaphors in these verses: first, the person who dresses in sheep's clothing to cover up a wolfish character, second, the good tree and the bad tree, each of which will bear fruit according to its nature, and third, the hypocrites who knew the name of the Lord but nothing else about him.

All three of these tell us that for spiritual and emotional health, there can be no disparity between the external and the internal. Our insides and our outsides have got to match.

Identity and self-esteem—knowing who we are and feeling good about ourselves—are essential for happy and serene living.

They go together. How can we feel good about ourselves if we don't know who we are? And once we've discovered our identity, we've got to believe that we are rare jewels with value and worth as persons created in the image of God.

It is out of this knowledge and acceptance of ourselves that self-worth emerges. It has nothing to do with position, class, prestige, or money. It is an attitude. It's how we *feel* about ourselves. We cannot give self-worth to somebody else, and no one else can give it to us. Other people may give us honor, respect, and power, but they cannot make us feel good about ourselves if we don't believe in ourselves.

A number of years ago I was invited for a private audience with the late emperor of Ethiopia, His Imperial Majesty, Haile Selassie. According to Ethiopian tradition, he was a descendant of the offspring from a dalliance between King Solomon and the Queen of Sheba. He had ascended to the throne of the ancient kingdom as a boy of seventeen and had become a legend during his reign of nearly half a century.

After arriving in the capital city of Addis Ababa, I was told to wait in my hotel room for a call from the royal palace. It came three days later! I never knew how much of the wait was really necessary and how much was calculated to put me in the proper frame of mind for my audience with this royal personage. During those three days I was given careful instruction on imperial protocol. I was told to bow on meeting the emperor but not to touch his royal person. I was not to cross my legs. On leaving, I must not turn my back, which meant that I had to navigate my exit by glancing behind me, making sure I didn't fall over any royal furniture.

When the summons finally came, I was taken to an anteroom where I waited for probably half an hour. A regally dressed guard stood at the door at all times, and once, on hearing him snap to attention and click his heels, I turned expecting to see a prince or visiting potentate emerge from the emperor's presence. Instead, out trotted a tiny chihuahua, the emperor's personal pet! At that moment, I felt like Rodney Dangerfield; the dog got more respect than I did.

Finally, it was my turn, and I found myself in the presence of a small man who appeared to be not much more than five feet tall. We talked for a while about matters of mutual interest. He was genial, pleasant, and shy. The shyness, it seemed to me, arose out of insecurity and uncertainty. I was reminded of the timid, fearful little man behind the fire-breathing mask who called himself the Wizard of Oz. Too unsure of himself to appear in his own skin, he sought the protection and security of a fearsome facade.

I wondered if much the same was not true of this man behind the medals and gold braid in Ethiopia's throne room who called himself the Lion of Judah. Having played a public role since he was a teenager, he had probably never had a chance to discover who he really was. All his life, courtiers had been making him into the person the royal role required him to be. Cringing behind the imperial mask was a scared little boy, I felt, unable to feel secure in himself because he didn't know who he was.

Others could give him the titles and privileges of royalty, but they couldn't give him self-worth. That comes only when there is substance behind the symbols.

I thought about that scene not long ago in a setting that was exactly the opposite. The location was a garbage dump just outside Monterrey, Mexico. There I met a woman worthy of being royalty. Beatriz was thirty-seven years old, and she had eleven children. She had been abandoned by her husband and had gone to live at the city's refuse dump, the only place where she could survive and hold her family together.

Her house was a small, one-room shelter made of flattened tin cans and tattered pieces of burlap. The smoke and stench from the mounds of burning garbage permeated the air, my clothing, the car upholstery, everything. Beatriz swept streets for the city and earned eighty dollars a month. Food for the family often came from what was scavenged from the dump.

In those circumstances it would have been easy to feel demeaned, worthless, and victimized. But this woman would not allow anyone to feel sorry for her. And there was no self-pity in her voice or manner. She was a survivor and wasn't the least bit ambivalent about her identity. Obviously, she didn't live under her circumstances; she lived on top of them. And at that time, her circumstances just happened to include a garbage dump. But it might as well have been a royal estate, for I left her home that day feeling that I had been with a queen. Her inside and her outside matched, and the combination produced a strength of character that commanded respect.

People judge by the outward appearance, the prophet Samuel was told, but God looks on the heart. The image the world sees and the reality that is open to God are two different things. All the metaphors that Jesus used in this part of the sermon have to do with pretense versus reality. In the same breath, he talks about healthy trees and sick trees, wolves pretending to be sheep, those who did miracles in his name but whom he turned away unrecognized. In no case did the inside and outside match.

Jesus is saying essentially the same thing when he talks about a divided kingdom, "Every kingdom divided against itself is laid waste, and no city or house divided against itself will stand" (Matt. 12:25). If our external image portrays a character that is not backed up by a conscious self founded on integrity, the "kingdom of the soul" will be ripped apart by the stress.

This idea is nowhere better illustrated than in Oscar Wilde's novel *The Picture of Dorian Gray*. The hero, Dorian, like Wilde himself, has no integrating factor in his life, so he is forced to contrive an identity. He must make himself up as he goes along. Half of him is characterized by decadence while the other half is unspoiled innocence, represented by his portrait. Like Narcissus, Dorian falls in love with his image instead of developing esteem for his real self.

Wilde describes him graphically: "The sense of his own beauty came on him like a revelation. . . . Yes, there would be a day when his face would be wrinkled and wizened, his eyes dim and colorless, the grace of his figure broken and deformed. . . . The life that was to make his soul would mar his body. He would become dreadful, hideous, and uncouth . . . but this picture will remain always young. He will never be older than this day of June . . .

if it were only the other way! If it were I who was to be always young and the picture that was to grow old! For that—for that—I would give everything! Yes, there is nothing in the whole world I would not give! I would give my soul for that!"[2]

And that is the way it happened. Dorian maintains his look of unspoiled innocence throughout a life of debauchery and deceit. Only the portrait of his soul shows the reality of what is happening. In the picture, "hideous lines seared the wrinkling forehead . . . crawled around the heavy sensual mouth . . . coarse bloated hands . . . the misshapen body and the failing limbs."

By the time Dorian tries to change, he cannot. His outside and inside have been at variance for so long that he is reduced to an empty, soulless existence. He has become a divided kingdom. Dorian decides he must take a knife to the canvas, since it is the true record of what he has become. All during his hypocritical life, he has kept the painting hidden away in a locked room. That is where his servants discover him: "When they entered they found, hanging upon the wall, a splendid portrait of their master as they had last seen him, in all the wonder of his exquisite youth and beauty. Lying on the floor was a dead man, in evening dress, with a knife in his heart. He was withered, wrinkled, and loathsome of visage."[3]

There was no integration of the soul, so Dorian was not able to withstand the destructive forces that tore away at him. Sadly, disintegration is a common experience for people today. There are no inner values to hold them together when the outer values crumble. That is why Jesus said these next words: "Therefore everyone who hears these words of mine and puts them into practice is like a wise man who built his house upon the rock. The rain came, the streams rose, and the winds blew and beat against that house; yet it did not fall, because it had its foundation on the rock" (Matt. 7:24-25, NIV).

This is a commentary on his teaching about wolves not pretending to be sheep, about healthy trees and good fruit, about honest prophets and true miracle workers. He's still talking about transparency and honesty and personal integrity in daily life. He wants us to hear his words and act on them so that we may bring the inside and outside into harmony with each other, and this we will do, he says, if we truly hear.

When we truly hear his words and act on them, we will have emotional stability, spiritual wholeness, and strength of character. There will be a rock-solid foundation under our lives.

We can have a stable foundation even in a garbage dump. Beatriz had a sense of identity and self-worth, and none of it depended on where she lived or how she earned a living. There is something very healthy about that attitude. If others cannot give us a feeling of self-worth, neither can they take it away. It is our God-given right to like ourselves, to believe in ourselves.

And why shouldn't we believe in ourselves? God believes in us! His word for us is yes! Paul words it this way, "He [God] has anointed us, set his seal of ownership on us, and put his Spirit in our hearts as a deposit, guaranteeing what is to come" (2 Cor. 1:21–22, NIV). What more could God do to affirm our worth? We are his creation, wonderful and rare, unique and special. And although it may sound trite, it is still true: God don't make no junk!

Much of our identity is tied to our names. My name establishes my personhood. This is not inconsequential. Actually, God seems to have started the business of establishing identity through names. He gave Adam a name, and it certainly wasn't meant just to keep from getting him mixed up with somebody else, because he was the only human being around at the time. Adam's name gave him identity just as he established the identity of the animals by naming them. Then Eve got a name, which means "the mother of all who live."

In the story Jesus told of the rich man and the beggar, the rich man is nameless, not because he is rich but because his self-centered life has distanced him from God. The beggar, however, Jesus identifies by name, Lazarus. The beggar's personhood is recognized, while the rich man remains an anonymous member of a social class.

This seems to go along with what Jesus had to say about the relationship between God and his people when, speaking of the

Good Shepherd, he says, "He calls his own sheep by name" (John 10:3). God never addresses any of us merely as "Hey, you!"

Now, in case you think I am making too much of an obscure point, let me give you something else to consider. When God was telling Job about the mysteries of creation, he said it all took place "while the morning stars sang together and all the angels shouted for joy" (Job 38:7, NIV). I puzzled over this burst of cosmic harmony until one day I read in the Psalms that God had "decided the number of the stars and calls each one of them by name" (147:4, TEV). I believe the stars sang on the discovery that they are not just anonymous specks in the night sky. Each has a name and an identity.

That's worth singing about.

Let me explain further why I have felt it important to make this point about names in connection with identity and self-worth. I have discovered that when I want to distance myself from someone, the first thing I do is diminish personhood by ignoring that person's name and assigning him or her to a group or class. That way I can be very impersonal and feel no need to establish a relationship.

If I take this diminishing of personhood to an extreme, I can even kill this person and feel next to nothing. That's why in a war we must categorize our enemies. They becomes "Japs" or "gooks" or "commies." The Russian fighter pilot who sent 269 people to their deaths when he shot down the Korean airliner wasn't, to his mind, killing fellow human beings. His last radio message was "The target is destroyed." Human life was just a blip on his radar screen.

People we want to hate or discriminate against become "Hymies" or "wops" or "honkies" or "wetbacks" or "niggers." We don't want to know them as persons, because we might find out, like Will Rogers, that "I never met a man I didn't like."

But when I acknowledge your name, it means I have seen you as a person. You have worth equal to my own. And that means I am already connected to you in a relationship that requires me to feel and care. I may treat you badly, but I can no longer feel good about it.

On the other hand, if I depersonalize you, I can treat you as I want to and feel no guilt. You are just a statistic in a faceless crowd. The Nazis certainly knew this; every Jew who came to a concentration camp was forced to have a number tattooed on the forearm. From that point on, the only relationship that existed was that of captive and captor.

Viktor Frankl, survivor of Auschwitz, tells about those who went to the gas ovens: "A definite number of prisoners had to go with each transport. It did not really matter which, since each of them was nothing but a number. . . . Any guard who wanted to make a charge against a prisoner just glanced at his number (and how we dreaded such glances!); he never asked for his name."[4]

Though we no longer have the gas ovens, I'm not sure how far we have come from that depersonalizing mentality. At a religious convention, a man walked up to a friend of mine, looked at his badge, and said, "Your name is familiar. What are you known for?" My friend was not seen as someone who might be worth getting to know. His identity was connected to his notoriety, his image, his public role. That attitude seems to be not too far beyond tattooing numbers on the forearm.

In the church community, we frequently use terms that cloak personhood. A new person who comes to church is a *prospect*. Then if that person makes a confession of faith, he or she is a *decision* or a *candidate for baptism*. Later, upon joining the church, this person becomes an *addition*. To the chairman of the stewardship committee, the new member is seen as a *giving unit*, and when he or she pledges, the treasurer assigns an *account number*. Only when the visitation minister makes a hospital call does the new member regain his or her name.

Talk about the loss of identity! I am not nearly as concerned as some people are about "whatever happened to the human race"— it is alive, although the vital signs are sometimes erratic—as I am about whatever happened to persons.

Now back to those Siamese twins of the inner search, identity and self-worth. Finding out who we are isn't especially easy and is always decidedly uncomfortable. Often it means stripping away layer after layer of old wallpaper, a distasteful task if ever there was one. It requires looking behind the mask at our uncertainty, our insecurity, our low self-esteem. It may even require admitting that we are like a piece of discount furniture—a few millimeters of mahogany veneer over sawdust.

If this is so, it means we have bought the Madison Avenue value system, which was described very succinctly in an article on the designer Ralph Lauren. According to this article at least, Lauren had this view of the world: "The crux of a person's identity, the experience of being that person, the aura of urbanity or erudition or sportsmanship that surrounds him, resides in the trappings, not in the person himself. There are shortcuts. . . . One needn't be well read, so long as one surrounds himself with books. One needn't play the piano, so long as one has a piano. In short, one can be whoever one wants to be. Or—more accurately—one can seem to be whoever one wants to be."[5]

According to that philosophy, it's quite OK to be a phony. In fact, you don't even need to bother with being real. That takes too long. Find the shortcuts. Style, not substance, is the ultimate criterion for judgment. So says the fashion guru Ralph Lauren.

Thomas Merton, a monk whose concern was the inner life, frequently spoke of the costly consequences of such a choice, "For me to be a saint means to be myself. God leaves us free to be whatever we like. We may be true or false; the choice is ours . . . but we cannot make these choices with impunity. Causes have effects, and if we lie to ourselves and to others, then we cannot expect to find truth and reality whenever we happen to want them."

When the former Beatle John Lennon lay on the backseat of a squad car, bleeding from the seven bullet wounds inflicted by his murderer, a policeman asked him the routine question, "Do you know who you are?" Lennon could just manage to nod before he died.

That may be a routine question for a policeman to ask a dying man, but for the rest of us it has radical consequences in the now. For that reason, I make three suggestions for discovering the real you.

First, develop a new kind of trust in God's presence and sovereign lordship in your life. At birth, he gives each of us a unique, authentic self. As we mature, God encourages us to discover that unique self he made each of us to be. He wants us to nurture it and then to let others see it as his handiwork.

But God will not force us on that inner journey. He leaves us free to be and become whatever we like. When we hide behind the mask of an altered image, it means that we are afraid others will not like us. This is where we have to trust God that the real self he gave us is as likable and as lovable as the self we pretend to be.

At a meeting of Alcoholics Anonymous, I picked up this plea for discovery and acceptance. The author is unknown, but it expresses what so many feel, addicted and nonaddicted alike.

> Don't be fooled by me.
> Don't be fooled by the face I wear.
> For I wear a thousand masks, masks that I'm afraid
> to take off, and none of them is me.
> Pretending is an art that's second nature to me,
> but don't be fooled . . . for God's sake, don't
> be fooled.
> I give the impression that I'm secure, that all is
> sunny and unruffled with me,
> within as well as without,
> that confidence is my name and coolness my game;
> and that I need no one.
> But don't believe me, please.
>
> My surface may seem smooth, but my surface is my
> mask.
> Beneath this lies no complacence.
> Beneath dwells the real me in confusion, in fear,
> and aloneness.
> But I hide this.
> I don't want anyone to know it.
> I panic at the thought of my weakness and fear of
> being exposed.
> That's why I frantically create a mask
> to hide behind,

a nonchalant, sophisticated facade,
to help me pretend, to shield me
from the glance that knows.

But such a glance is precisely my salvation. My only
salvation.
And I know it.
That is, if it's followed by acceptance, if it's
followed by love.
It's the only thing that will assure me of what
I can't assure myself . . .
that I am worth something.
But I don't tell you this. I don't dare.
I'm afraid to.
I'm afraid you'll think less of me, that you'll
laugh at me, and your laugh will kill me.
I'm afraid that deep down I'm nothing,
that I'm no good
and that you will see this and reject me.
So I play my game, my desperate game,
with a facade of assurance without,
and a trembling child within.
And so begins the parade of masks, and my life
becomes a front.
But don't be fooled by me.

Trust God that the real human you he made is at least as lovable, probably even more so, than the phony image of perfection that you hide behind.

Second, disclose yourself to others. There is no other way we can come to know ourselves. Plutarch quoted the Delphic oracle as wisely saying, "Know thyself." To me that always sounded cryptic and vague. I asked what seemed to me the logical question, "How can I know myself?" Experience has taught me the answer: "Make yourself known, and then you will know yourself."

It is in revealing ourselves to others that we get to know ourselves. But transparency is so scary that our true selves will emerge only when we sense love, trust, and acceptance. Self-disclosure is so crucial to emotional wholeness, however, that each of us needs to search to find that loving place where we can be accepted, warts and all.

Several years ago, after a lifetime of public ministry, I decided to quit reinventing myself to fit the image others wanted me to be. I had grown weary of being a symbol, a trademark, a spokesman. Only with the help of sensitive friends and the gentle leading of the Holy Spirit was I able to begin the inner search for the authentic self God made me to be.

As my self-acceptance has increased, my self-esteem has grown, until today I can say that, basically, I like the real person I am better that I did the public image I was striving to maintain.

Third, let what you do arise out of who you are. Being is more important than doing. As for me, I have decided that whatever I do for the rest of my life, it will not be in order to have an identity. It will be the result of allowing my God-given self to emerge. I'm done with posturing for a public that demands an unattainable and hypocritical perfection.

Jesus is the model for us all. Early in his life, he told the Pharisees, "I know where I came from and where I am going" (John 8:14, LB). He had a clear and certain fix on who he was, and the storms never broke him.

When Jesus was taken before the high priest who asked, "What do you have to say for yourself?" he did not answer a word.

Wrong question.

Later when the high priest asked if he was the Son of God, Jesus replied, "I am."

Right question, translated, "Do you know who you are?"

When Pilate asked him, "Are you the King of the Jews?" Jesus answered, "Yes, it is as you say."

Again, the right question.

But Luke says that when Herod "asked Jesus question after question, there was no reply." They were all the wrong questions, and never was there more dignity and authority in silence.[6]

Years ago, Toyohiko Kagawa, a saintly Japanese Christian who spent his life in sacrificial service to the poor in his country, was speaking at Princeton Seminary. A professor took one of his students to hear the gentle Kagawa. His talk was simple and basic.

When Dr. Kagawa was finished, the student turned to his professor and remarked, "He didn't say much, did he?"

In response the professor replied, "When you're hanging on a cross, you don't have to say anything."

When you are on a cross, unless your life validates your words, there is no witness. And that may well be the ultimate test for matching up the inside with the outside.

7. The Myth of Being Perfect

The children of a very prominent family decided to give their father a book of the family's history for a birthday present. To ensure that it would be well done, they commissioned a professional biographer. They warned him, however, about Uncle George, who had been the black sheep in the family.

"Uncle George was executed in the electric chair for murder," they said, "so maybe you should avoid mentioning him."

The biographer assured them he could hide Uncle George in such a way that he wouldn't embarrass anyone. When asked how he would do that, the writer said, "Oh, I'll just say that Uncle George occupied a chair of applied electronics at an important government institution. And then I'll say that he was attached to his position by the strongest of ties and that death came as a real shock."

Most of us don't have any ancestral skeletons in our family closets that need covering up, but a great many of us are playing games trying to hide our flawed humanity behind a facade of pretended perfection.

I have no trouble believing in a God who is perfect, without flaw or blemish. I need my Supreme Being to possess all those qualities that we normally associate with deity. To me, such a God is much more believable and appealing than those cavorting Greek mythological divinities on Mount Olympus who mocked people's weaknesses by playing tricks on them.

It comforts and stabilizes my faith to confess with the apostle James that in the God I know, there is no variation or hidden shadow. But I confess that I am perplexed and just a little angry when I am told that I, a mere mortal, must emulate all those wonderful qualities of perfection that I happily ascribe to God.

Yet that seems to be exactly what Jesus does in that troubling statement from the Sermon on the Mount in which he says, "You must be perfect—just as your Father in heaven is perfect" (Matt. 5:48, TEV).

That one is enough to bring everybody on the dance floor to a stumbling stop . . . and it generally does. I have heard an infinite number of interpretations, none of which fully satisfied me. They range from "that's the ideal but Jesus knows we can't attain it" to "God sees as perfect all those who are in Christ."

Since I couldn't relate to it in any practical way, I always sped past that verse. I didn't know what to make of it. I thought that anything as idealistic and unreachable as that must be nothing more than high-sounding rhetoric or hyberbole.

Attempting to make that point with his audience, one preacher asked them, "Is there anyone here who is perfect?" When no one volunteered, he followed up with a second question: "Have you ever heard of anyone who was perfect?"

A shy man nervously raised his hand, and the preacher asked him to identify this rare specimen he had heard about. "My wife's first husband!" the timid man responded.

Probably the first husband was not as perfect as his wife's memory was short, but let's agree that in order to understand this verse and the principle underlying it, we need to correct a flawed image of what it means to be perfect.

If it means to be without fault or error, then we are all in deep trouble. But how can it possibly mean that when in other places in the New Testament we are told that "all have sinned and come short of the glory of God" and "There is none who does good, no, not one?" These descriptions of the fallibility of human character fly in the face of our usual understanding of perfection.

We use the word *perfect* to describe diametric opposites. When a gymnast turns in a flawless performance during the Olympic games, we say, "That was a perfect ten." The term is defined by the context. On the other hand, the wife of a man who has had too much to drink at a party assures him on the way home that he made a "perfect fool" of himself. Certainly she doesn't mean he is without fault. In fact, in her eyes at that moment he doesn't possess a single redeeming quality.

Same word. Different application.

We may also say something is perfect when it is mature, complete, and fulfilling its intended purpose. A farmer surveying a ripening field of grain will say, "That is a perfect field of wheat." The farmer is not endorsing every stalk and every kernel but is pleased that earlier efforts are coming to fruition.

So how shall we understand what Jesus is telling us about being perfect? The Greek word here carries with it the idea of culmination, of maturity, of achievement in function, of something in good working order.

Ben Campbell Johnson's paraphrase of that verse adds considerable illumination: "My final adominition to you is to be fully man as God is fully God."[1]

I can understand that goal and even begin to take small steps toward reaching it—to be as fully human, which is all that God made me to be, as Yahweh is fully God. That means I can allow God to be God and I can get on with my full-time occupation of being human.

That makes sense to me, a lot more sense than striving for an unreal and unreachable perfection. There's a wonderful line by the English novelist Josephine Tey, creator of the detective Miss Pym, in one of her books, "My hairdresser, who lectures to me while he is doing my hair, says that one should allow everyone three faults. If one makes that allowance, one finds that the rest is surprisingly nice, he says."

What a redemptive way to see the imperfections of others and to have our own shortcomings viewed. Try that on yourself, your spouse, your children, your friends, and the people you work with. Allow yourself and them three faults each. Accept the fact that you and they are merely human, and see if you aren't a lot more relaxed. In fact, before long you will probably stop counting anyone's faults!

But many of us seem to need another image of ourselves—one that we can not only project before the public but also nurture in the privacy of our own souls. This image may be of the person we wish we were, or, even worse, secretly believe we are. It is an image that supports the myth of our moral superiority, even perfection.

Apart from its being false, another problem with this notion is that, with it, we make ourselves the yardstick for measuring everyone else's attitudes and actions. This sickness of perfectionism has at least three troubling consequences.

First, the myth of being perfect creates a counterfeit person, not an authentic one. An old preacher down South said it this way: "Be who you is, because if you ain't who you is, then you is who you ain't." Translation: If you're not real, then you're a fake. There is no middle ground between genuine and counterfeit.

When Jesus told us to be perfect as God is perfect, it wasn't a command to be super-Christian. That would be as ludicrous as the mild-mannered reporter Clark Kent stepping into a telephone booth, changing costumes, and coming out as Superman ready to fly over cities and catch speeding bullets with his bare hands. By its very dishonesty and self-deception that myth overlaid on the Christian experience betrays the principle of wholeness and maturity that Jesus encourages in his view of perfection.

Further, this distorted idea of perfectionism reveals a serious spiritual blindness in reality that has deep consequences. This is not a harmless little game of make-believe we are playing. It deals with the very life of the soul, the central core of our being. It has to do with basic truth, with having an honest evaluation of ourselves and with being able to distinguish reality from fantasy.

C. S. Lewis was heard to say one time, "The worst temptation is the temptation to virtue, not evil: A virtue that goes unchecked is much more dangerous than a blatant evil. A blatant evil makes you feel guilty, but a virtue makes you feel proud."

That is what got the Pharisees into trouble. They started to believe their own publicity. That's dangerous for anybody, especially when your own news releases portray you as 99.9 percent pure gold. Here is what Jesus told the people, "If your eyes are sound, [if you can view yourself honestly], your whole body will be full of light; but if your eyes are not good [if you have a distorted image of yourself] . . . the light in you is darkness [and] how terribly dark it will be!" (Matt. 6:22–23, TEV). The most terrible darkness is that of self-willed dishonesty, for it is the most difficult blindness to heal.

It was this self-deluding blindness of which the Pharisees were guilty. Jesus has a lot to say in the Sermon on the Mount and elsewhere about the Pharisees. His main quarrel with them was not that they were sinners but that they concealed their true identity behind masks and refused to acknowledge who they were.

Contrast his scorn for the Pharisees with his gentleness toward honest sinners—people like Zacchaeus and the immoral woman and the Samaritan adulteress and the publican at prayer whose only plea was "God, be merciful to me, a sinner."

Perhaps you share my belief that we need to reassess our overriding concern with the sins of the flesh—the ones easily seen and named—and our uncritical acceptance of those sins of the spirit that Jesus seems to emphasize. The sins of the spirit are those that strike at the vitals of the soul because they rob us of our authentic self and replace it with a worthless, counterfeit person. Yet we tend to regard these sins of the spirit as not nearly as bad as lying, stealing, or sleeping around.

Would Jesus endorse that attitude? Not likely, since that is the hypocrisy he condemned so severely. In his famous seven woes pronounced on the Pharisees, Jesus lays bare their spiritual malignancy like a surgeon. His words are the scalpel, "Woe to you, scribes and Pharisees, hypocrites! For you cleanse the outside of the cup and of the plate, but inside they are full of extortion and rapacity . . . you who are like whitewashed tombs, which outwardly appear beautiful but within they are full of dead men's bones and uncleanness" (Matt. 23:25, 27; Luke 11:39-40).

This is Jesus' description of the so-called perfect people who paraded themselves as examples of what God wanted the rest of us to be like. But Jesus called them "hypocrites," a word used to describe actors who perform behind a mask to signify the role they are playing. They do not reveal their true identity. Appearing to be respectful and virtuous, role players live safe and unexposed behind the mask, never venturing off the stage to face life with all its risks, its rough-and-tumble, its innumerable chances for failure.

These counterfeit people may have started out innocently enough playing a role, but they ended up living the lie. Dietrich Bonhoeffer said, "Many Christians are unthinkably horrified when a real sinner is discovered among the righteous. So we remain alone in our sin, living in lies and hypocrisy."[2]

For perfectionists, failure is the one unthinkable experience. It would confirm their worst fears about themselves, that in spite of their achievements, they are still phony. Recent studies have identified an "imposter syndrome," a phenomenon that affects a surprisingly large percentage of high achievers. These are perfectionists, who need to always perform flawlessly and can't accept praise for what they have already done because they keep thinking they won't be able to measure up to past performance.

Such perfectionists equate failure with shame and humiliation and are driven by the erroneous belief that as long as they are in control, they can prevent mistakes. So they can't relax, they experience stress and burnout, their health and relationships suffer, and the authentic self that God created is killed off in favor of a false image they cling to for the sake of pride. All is sacrificed on the altar of a myth—the myth of perfection.

And still we keep on trying to play God, when the most he wants from us is for us to be perfectly human.

To acknowledge the truth about ourselves and accept our vulnerability takes enormous courage. But the reward is great; this truth is at least a part of the truth that Jesus said would set us free.

A young woman was filling out her college entrance form, and her heart sank when she came to this question, Are you a leader? Being truthful, she wrote no and with a heavy heart returned the form. To her surprise, she received a letter from the Admissions Office that read something like this, "A study of the applications reveals that this year our college will have 1,826 leaders. Therefore, we are accepting you because we feel it is imperative that they have one follower."

To be honest about oneself is certainly part of what it means to be fully human as God is fully God. The French philosopher Blaise Pascal wrote: "We strive continually to adorn and preserve our imaginery self, neglecting the true one." Meanwhile, inside us, there is our private self that cries out for recognition that it, too, exists and that it is the real person, not created in our own flawed self-image but made in the perfect image of God.

There is a second troubling consequence of perfectionism: the myth of being perfect produces unrealistic expectations of others, and thus disappointment.

We return to Jesus' implacable enemies, the Pharisees, for an example. They demanded that everyone else live up to their self-imposed standards of conduct, but they conveniently ignored their own moral lapses. Jesus warns the people against them, "Do not, however, imitate their actions because they don't practice what they preach. They tie onto people's backs loads that are heavy and hard to carry, yet they aren't willing even to lift a finger to help them carry those loads" (Matt. 23:3-4, TEV).

The Pharisees wanted conformity to their standards. Jesus was content to accept people as they were, while always encouraging them to be true to their higher calling as children of their heavenly Father. But he never expected or asked more from others than their humanity allowed them to freely give.

I have such trouble learning to live with the humanity and weakness of others. If only I could be as generous and forgiving of their failures as I am of my own! But when I change the focus from myself to others, my standards of judgment suddenly escalate. I project onto them the perfction that is impossible for me, knowing full well that I will only be disappointed because my expectations are unrealistic and unattainable.

Probably the greatest transgressors in this respect are parents who inflict these demands on their chldren. My own children could never be as good as I insisted they should be. It now amazes me that I ever thought they could, because they came out of the loins of my own imperfect humanity.

Do you remember the point of William Shakespeare's tragic play King Lear? In the first scene, Lear calls his three daughters and tells them he wants to retire and divide his power among them. But first he demands that each of them swear her unchanging love for him.

Two of them are quick to give the old king the glib assurance he asks for. Goneril flatters his ego with her words: "Sire, I love you more than words can yield the matter, dearer than eyesight, space and liberty, beyond what can be valued, rich or rare."

Cordelia, the third daughter and her father's favorite, cannot bring herself to say more than honesty and human limitation will permit. She is convinced that her relationship with her father already establishes her devotion, so she says simply: "I love your majesty according to my bond; no more, no less."

Her assertion of honest filial affection should have been enough, but Lear wants more, so he disowns Cordelia and gives the power to the other two. But it isn't long until, predictably, they turn on their father, deprive him of his knights who protect him, and strip him of his dignity. He goes mad, sick at heart over their betrayal, which any observer of human nature could have predicted. Lear himself had set it up by demanding more than a human being could deliver.

In spite of her father's madness, Cordelia returns to him and reestablishes her bond with him. She had made him no false promises, and if Lear had not set up unrealistic expectations based on the myth of human perfectability, he might have been spared a tragedy.

Jesus offers a dramatic contrast. Knowing what was in the human heart, Jesus was able to accept the limitations of all his disciples, including Judas's betrayal and Peter's denial, and still love them with an undiminished love. Or, as the apostle John puts it, "Having loved his own who were in the world, he loved them to the end" (John 13:1).

One of the most gentle encounters in the Bible occurs following Peter's denial. After the resurrection, Jesus comes to a few of the disciples on the seashore early in the morning and asks for Peter's affirmation of love. He asks three times, corresponding to the number of Peter's denials, but each time he changes the tone of the question.

It was Peter who had impetuously promised to remain loyal even though all the others might abandon Jesus. Now in the presence of the others around the breakfast fire that morning, Jesus asks Peter, "Do you love me more than these?" using a very strong verb for the word we translate "love."

But Peter has experienced the humbling reality of his humanity, and he can no longer speak of comparative love. So he uses another verb with a slightly different meaning, "You know that I have affection for you."

In his reply, Jesus acknowledges that Peter has changed the verb, but he still presses the point. In essence, he says, "Now dropping all comparisions, do you really love me?" and repeats the same strong word for love he had used previously.

Humbled by the memory of his failure, Peter gives the same answer as before, "You know that I have affection for you." He still doesn't dare affirm that he possesses this higher kind of love. The third time Jesus asks the question, with deep tenderness he accepts Peter's human limitations on his ability to love. Once the rash and hasty disciple has himself acknowledged it, Jesus then adopts Peter's own words –"affection"– and affirms that it is enough.

Do we need any further evidence that it is just the way Jesus says it is – his yoke is easy and his burden light? He lays no weight on us that we cannot bear. The crushing weight comes when I, like the Pharisees, lay my own demands on top of what Jesus asks.

Jesus does not demand that we be perfect in love, perfect in living, perfect in attitude. It is enough for Christians to say what recovering alcoholics say about themselves, "We claim spiritual progress, not spiritual perfection." We should make no demands on others that Jesus does not make. He accepts even our humbler, more subjective love, for that too is precious when it is not coerced but freely and joyously given.

There is yet a third way in which perfectionism leads to trouble. The myth of being perfect negates a need for the grace of God. Let's face it, the Pharisees did not feel any need for God's grace and mercy. They thought they were doing quite well on their own. That's why they could be so harsh with others without being aware of any inconsistency. Feeling no need for grace themselves, why should they show tenderness or forgiveness toward other people?

The name of the game they played was judgment—swift, harsh, and unrelenting. The Pharisees as a sect may have passed off the stage of history, but their perfectionist, tight-lipped attitude is present all too often in Christian circles today.

In 1982, I entered into a personal experience that was, by any comparison, the most painful and distressing I had ever known. I risk sharing it, not because it is unique, but hoping that it may be helpful to someone else who is struggling.

After more than thirty years of preaching grace as a doctrine, I never understood how badly I needed it myself on a daily basis until my life fell off the pages of the Bible.

What I mean is this: As long as I was safely within the boundaries of social conformity, I didn't seem to need grace. Grace means "undeserved favor," and everybody was telling me how dedicated and sacrificial and self-giving I was. But they didn't know just how much personal insecurity my mask was covering up. They said if anybody deserved God's blessing on his life, it was somebody who went out binding up bodies and saving souls. To "them" I was an evangelist-humanitarian. The mask had served its purpose well.

It became awfully easy to believe those press releases. I can tell you that it isn't hard to get infected with the superstar syndrome that runs through so many Christian movements today like a contagion.

But then the image of my perfection was shattered. Marital breakup was followed by career loss and abandonment by colleagues and friends. I felt panic, uncertainty, self-doubt. A small group of colleagues who had pledged themselves to a pastoral ministry in my life suddenly had nothing "pastoral" to say. My life lay in little pieces outside the safe parameters for a so-called Christian leader. I learned in the most painful way that there is no greater sin for a Christian leader than to allow his or her clay feet to show.

I have decided this is true because it shakes the fragile world of pretense in which so many people live. In the mirror of another's failure, we must, at least for a brief moment, see a glimpse of our own imperfection.

But it was not until I reached this extremity in my life—what I call falling off the pages of the Bible—that I experienced grace in a way understandable for me. I know that I have received God's grace at many other times in my life, but it was then that I was most keenly aware of being emotionally touched and sustained by it. When the image of perfection slipped and the whole world saw the flawed creature behind the mask—in that naked moment—God's grace meant the most to me.

It is only when we are no longer enamored of the myth of our own goodness that we are ready for the coming of the grace of God.

In one of his classic fantasy stories, *The Great Divorce*, C. S. Lewis attempts to set forth the contrast between heaven and hell. There is an odd scene in which he describes a busload of people from the Grey City of Hell being taken to the entrance of heaven. They are offered admission to heaven, but with one exception, they all refuse it.

The people in heaven, whom Lewis calls "Solid Persons," are so radiant and so substantial that they make the visitors from hell look like mere shadows. The one pale ghost from hell who makes an excursion into heaven is met by one of the Solid People. To his dismay, the ghost discovers that at one time on earth, this Solid Person had worked for him. But what rankled even more was that the Solid Person had in his time on earth actually committed a murder. The pale ghost was astonished that he was in hell while the man who had been a murderer was in heaven.

"Look at me, now," he complained. "I gone straight all my life. I don't say I was a religious man and I don't say I had no faults, far from it. But I done my best all my life, see? . . . That's the sort of chap I was. I never asked for anything that wasn't mine by rights. If I wanted a drink I paid for it and if I took my wages I done my job, see? . . . I'm asking for nothing but my rights . . . I'm not asking for anybody's bleeding charity."

The Solid Person looked at the grey ghost and gave this thoughtful answer, "Then do. At once. Ask for the Bleeding Charity."[3]

Hell, whatever it is and wherever it is, will be populated by people who thought they could live life by themselves. They were certain they were good enough to get into heaven by asserting their rights. In reality, they never understood how much they needed grace.

That is the final tragedy of the myth—no, the sin—of perfectionism. It is to have missed the grace of God that alone can gain us entrance and make us one of the Solid Persons. Only admitted sinners need apply. All others will be rejected.

"My final admonition to you," Jesus said, "is to be fully man as God is fully God."

With our first timid steps outside the myth, we may seem as graceless as a penguin doing the rhumba. But at least we'll experience the joy of dancing our own step instead of feeling like a stiff-legged stork that is afraid to let go and be the bird God made it to be.

8. What to Do with the Other You

Suzanne was married when she was eighteen, and for twenty-four years had been a loving and faithful wife. That's the role she was taught to play—submissive, quiet, dutiful. She had no identity apart from that of wife and mother.

She was married to a tyrant. Sam was a mean man. He grew up in a violent environment, was abused as a child, and had always kept his feelings to himself. He was a textbook case: resentful and abusive, a seething volcano inside, pouring out lava through psychological fissures but careful to keep the cap on any major eruption.

Suzanne got most of his lava. He would embarrass her in public, put her down in front of the children, and sometimes physically abuse her. She stuffed it inside for twenty-four years, playing her role of loyal wife and obedient servant. When anyone said, "How are you, Suzanne? And how is Sam?" she would smile and say, "Fine. We're doing just fine, thank you."

It happened on Super Bowl Sunday. Sam and the boys were watching the football game on television. Suzanne was in the kitchen, preparing the meal by herself and about ready to slice the ham she'd just taken from the oven. Sam, who had been drinking beer, came through the doorway, grabbed her, and threw her against the counter as he yelled, "When in the hell are we going to eat, anyway?"

Suzanne's reaction was instantaneous. Before she or Sam knew what was happening, the knife was deep in his chest, plunged there with the full force of her being. When the family came in she was staring down at the lifeless body, saying over and over again, "My God, what have I done?"

We know what happened, of course. Resentment and rage, denied and repressed for nearly a quarter of a century, finally had broken out of the cellar where Suzanne had kept her dark side locked away. In one stroke, she not only murdered her husband but her own perceived innocence. Suzanne had never admitted that she had a shadow side, and it ultimately did her in.

With variations, the story could be written countless times. But what does such a sordid theme have to do with dancing on the strait and narrow? Just this: As long as we are under the tyranny of the other self, which the Swiss psychologist Carl Jung called our "shadow side," we can never know the freedom and fullness of joy that Jesus wants to give us as Kingdom people.

There are more than a few places in the Sermon on the Mount where Jesus encourages us to face our shadow side. His teachings are never one-dimensional. He touches many levels — social, ethical, psychological, as well as spiritual. Even while he's telling us stories, he's trying to teach us about life. Often he uses a rhetorical device called hyberbole, which means to exaggerate something to the point of making it ludicrous for dramatic effect.

That's what Jesus is doing when he talks about the speck or "mote" in someone else's eye and the log or "beam" in our own eye, "Why, then, do you look at the speck in your brother's eye and pay no attention to the log in your own eye? How dare you say to your brother, 'Please, let me take that speck out of your eye,' when you have a log in your own eye? You hypocrite! First take the log out of your own eye, and then you will be able to see clearly to take the speck out of your brother's eye." (Matt. 7:3–5, TEV).

Can you see how absurd it is to try to find a speck in the eye of your brother or sister while your vision is obstructed by the log in your own eye? It's a joke, like the one Jesus made about adding "a single hour to his life" by worry (Matt. 6:27, NIV). It's preposterous, yet Jesus knows it describes our behavior. We overlook our own lumberyard while searching for dust specks in the eye of another, or we offer to heal someone else when we are terminally ill from the same disease.

Most often what we see in the eye of someone else is a projection of our own dark side, and Jesus is telling us to deal with our own shadow before we start looking for flaws in others. Else what does it mean when Jesus tells us not to judge, because we will get the same judgment we give? "Do not judge others, so that God will not judge you, for God will judge you in the same way you judge others, and he will apply to you the same rules you apply to others" (Matt. 7:12–2, TEV).

Is Jesus telling us we should not use our critical faculties to make objective evaluations? That doesn't seem to fit the context. Rather, he is advising us that any evaluation we make should be free of our own shadow projection, for we often hate in others what we refuse to judge in ourselves. It is not that God is keeping score, just waiting to give us tit for tat, but a spiritual law that says that we will face our own inner judgment if we stand in judgment on others. In that sense, our judgment of others always returns to us, because in judging them, we are in effect, judging ourselves. It is as if Jesus is saying, "Come to terms with the shadow within yourself so you may avoid the sin of projecting it on others."

Let's look now at another teaching from the Sermon on the Mount. This one is about hating our enemies (Matt. 5:43–47). Whatever else is wrong with hating (and there is plenty), certainly one danger is that we tend to become like what we oppose.

So acknowledging our shadow side has a great deal to do with experiencing the freedom that is potentially ours when we enter the Kingdom. When we refuse to own our shadow as a part of us, we are in its thrall and grip. Then it is more our master than our servant, and, as such, it has power to deny us freedom and to keep us from the dance. As uncomfortable and unpleasant as it may be to acknowledge our shadow side as our own, we will ultimately pay a far heavier price if we disown it.

There is hope for us if we can be as candid as that comic strip possum, Pogo. After one particularly spicy encounter with some animals outside his home in the Okefenokee swamp of south Georgia, Pogo announced, "We have met the enemy, and he is us."

There is hope when we can recognize the enemy within because as Jung points out, there can be no shadow without a light. Thank God for the light! We are not all darkness. The shadow is by nature and definition the opposite of the brighter side of our personality, the one we proudly show to the public. The shadow is primitive, instinctive, animalistic.

The shadow is everything the brighter side doesn't want to be. Or it also may be true to say that it is everything we would like to be but don't dare. The shadow is not only what we don't want others to know about us, it is also what we have conveniently "forgotten" about ourselves through denial and repression. It is that part of us that lusts, lies, hates, deceives, alienates, and seems incapable of redemption.

The apostle Paul recognized his own shadow and quite openly acknowledged its presence within, "For even though the desire to do good is in me, I am not able to do it. I don't do the good I want to do; instead, I do the evil I do not want to do" (Rom. 7:18–19, TEV). Then, in discomfort and despair, he cries out on behalf of us all, "What an unhappy man I am! Who will rescue me from this body that is taking me to death?" (Rom. 7:24, TEV).

Or to ask the question another way: What can you do with the other you? There are, it seems, four possible options.

The first is license. Some people deal with the shadow by allowing it to have its own way. They do not have the moral courage to face down the depravity of their own dark souls, so they turn freedom into license. Claiming to be liberated from the inhibitions and taboos of society, they act out their dark passions in the name of "letting it all hang out."

As a result, we have pedophiles, wife-beaters, con artists, drug dealers, arsonists, kidnappers, embezzlers, and all the rest in the catalog of revolting social aberrations.

The people who engage in this unacceptable and embarrassing behavior are also known as movie stars, clergymen, company presidents, lawyers, schoolteachers, truck drivers, stockbrokers. It is in such people and in ordinary folks like you and me – in other words, in us all – that the light and shadow side meet. And from time to time, the shadow is allowed to take over the driver's seat.

When Gary, the eldest son of Bing Crosby, was forty-nine years old, he revealed that the old crooner had been an abusive father who beat his sons. "My father would come home at six o-clock," he said, "and by 6:05 he'd heard the news of what I'd done. Then I'd get bent over and my pants taken down and beat until I bled." Gary went on to say that he and his three brothers endured the pain and abuse by dreaming up ways of murdering their father.

A lot of people were shocked by Gary's revelations. We weren't surprised when Joan Crawford's daughter pulled back the curtain on her private life. After all, how can anybody who played all those bitchy roles be expected to come home from a hard day at the studio and act like Mommie Dearest? But in our eyes, Bing was different. He was the kindly priest, the genial golfer, and all the white Christmases rolled into one. How we saw him was the way makeup and public relations artists, script writers and directors of Tinseltown presented him. Apparently, the real Bing was not all wool, but partly polyester, and quite a bit less than a yard wide.

And a lot of people wish that Gary had just kept it all in the family. It was very disillusioning. If the mellowest among us didn't make it, what hope is there for us lesser mortals?

Well, there is hope, and it is this: honesty about our own duality frees us from the tyranny of the shadow. Being liberated, we are now free to choose the higher path. But we must make the right choices in the testing times.

Despite the fact that God gave King Saul a new nature when Samuel anointed him (1 Sam. 10:9), Saul lived with a brooding shadow inside him. In various translations it is called a "familiar spirit," "an evil spirit from the Lord," a "distressing spirit," and a "tormenting spirit from the Lord" (1 Sam. 19:9). It is scarcely debatable that this was the king's shadow side, to which he increasingly gave license for evil.

Evil done in the name of religion is as scary to me as anarchy and terrorism, because all represent unrestrained self-will. Religious fanatics who have indulged their shadow side have brought us such nightmares as the Inquisition, the Ku Klux Klan, extreme Zionism, holy wars, Nazism, the insanity in northern Ireland, and the bombing of abortion clinics. Laurens Van der Post, who wrote numerous novels out of his South African experience, summed it up this way: "Human beings are perhaps never more frightening than when they are convinced beyond doubt that they are right." If you think that applies only to Shi'ite Muslim mullahs from Iran, think again.

I refuse to join any religious posse that rides forth to dispense frontier justice in the name of God, because I know how many demons are waiting to be unchained in the name of somebody's perverted truth. Besides, lynch mobs make lousy dance partners.

It matters little whether unrestrained indulgence is carried on in the name of religion or in the name of personal freedom. Unleashing the shadow side is a terribly destructive way to deal with it. Without godly restraint, the shadow rampages and destroys, always revealing the demonic. Allowing our shadow to have free reign never enhances true freedom. And anytime we turn the shadow side loose with a hunting license, both we and society pay a terrible price.

A second way to handle one's shadow side is denial. Many people who would reject license as a way of handling the shadow side are ready to endorse denial as acceptable. Yet pretending we have no shadow is perhaps the most dishonest of all approaches. It flies in the face of our own experience and ignores the reality we know. How else can we possibly explain cases like Suzanne and Sam and thousands more that defy rational explanation?

It isn't enough to pass it off with, "The devil made me do it." To bring it even closer to home, how else do you explain the delicious tremor that runs through us all—a feeling that we are ashamed to admit even to ourselves—when we hear about some scandal or aberrant behavior?

Denial is a game that won't work any better than license. William Miller makes the point well when he writes, "Closing your eyes in the darkness neither increases your safety nor improves your vision."[1]

As threatening and distasteful as it is to own up to our shadow side, we are at greater risk if we do not. The more we deny it, the more power we give it. Since we are unwilling or unable to admit those feelings and attitudes, what finally happens is that we turn to a defense mechanism. We do what we always do with something we don't want; we throw it away.

Psychologically, that translates into projection, because we can't physically throw away our attitudes. Instead, what we do is project them onto another person so we may deal with them without having to face ourselves. That person then becomes devilish and sinister in our eyes because we hate in him or her what we refuse to recognize in ourselves.

Does that help us see why Jesus was such a threat to the Pharisees and why they hated him with such intensity? He challenged their perceived goodness. They started to suspect that Jesus saw through them when he told the people that their righteousness had to go deeper than that of the Parisees or they would never see the kingdom of heaven.

Another way to put it would be, "Don't project your sins and failures on others as the Pharisees do. Admit that your shadow belongs to you, and you weaken its power over you. Then you can begin to act righteously, or from right motives."

My spiritual and psychological wholeness is critically related to how I deal with my shadow side. I cannot be a whole person until I accept my inner opponent as a legitimate part of my personality. And only when I stop projecting the less attractive parts of my personality on others am I free to own them as a part of me.

No matter what name we give it, denial doesn't solve the problem.

A family moved to a new city, and the only son was lonely in the new neighborhood. So he got his pet and went for a walk, hoping to find a friend. Instead, he met the local gang.

The bully in the gang wanted to establish his authority over the newcomer so he threatened the boy if he didn't join their gang. Then he noticed the boy's pet and said, "That's the ugliest dog I've ever seen! Yellow, beady-eyed, short-tailed, long-nosed, and stumpy-legged! Why, it's ridiculous! If you don't join our gang tomorrow, I'm not only going to beat you up, but I'm going to turn my dog, Killer, loose on yours."

They met again the next day, and the new boy declined to join the gang, so the leader unleashed his huge German shepherd. "Get him, Killer!" he yelled, "get that ugly, yellow, beady-eyed, short-tailed, long-nosed, stumpy-legged mutt!" So the huge German shepherd circled the boy's pet a couple of times and then lunged at him. But the new kid's pet opened the largest mouth you ever saw and swallowed Killer in one gulp.

The gang members were horrified. They'd never seen anything like that before. Finally, the leader said to the new boy, "What kind of dog is that ugly, yellow, beady-eyed, short-tailed, long-nosed, stumpy-legged thing anyway?"

The young boy responded, "I don't know, but before we cut off his tail and painted him yellow, he was an alligator!"

Even if we try denying our shadow side or call it something else, we've still got an alligator in our basement, green or yellow, tail or no tail.

A third favorite way for many Christians to deal with their shadow side is to try and suppress it. If giving it unrestrained license is unthinkable and denying it is for all practical purposes impossible, then what are we to do with this unruly part of our personality that has the power to embarrass us and cause all kinds of trouble?

Often my solution is to push it back into the swamp with all the other creatures. Keep it hidden. Suppress it. Don't ever let it show its real face. But as Professor Jung once said, "Mere suppression of the shadow is as little of a remedy as beheading would be for a headache."

But, somebody protests, "Isn't it better to let sleeping dogs lie?" Only if the sleeping dogs never wake up. Given the nature of a suppressed shadow, I wouldn't risk much money on that.

Billy was just a little boy when his father died. His mother told him that now he had to be especially good because there were just the two of them and she wouldn't be able to handle any trouble. So Billy became very good—almost too good to be true.

It wasn't long before his mother remarried. Billy thought it was too soon, but he was still a good boy—never caused any trouble, was a fine student, went to church, was always quiet and well-mannered. All the other mothers said to their sons, "Why can't you be like Billy?" He never tested the limits like most teenagers; he carefully controlled his behavior to do only what he thought his mother and the community expected him to do. And he did it not to impress anybody, but because he believed it was right.

One evening when he was fifteen, Billy got ready for bed and turned on the television in his room. After watching for a few minutes, he picked up a souvenir machete given to him by a cousin. He called his mother to come to his room, and as she entered, he struck her with the machete. The next few minutes were like a horror movie. Later he was found wandering the streets with no memory of what had happened.

Do you know what the neighbors said? "Some other kid maybe, but not Billy." "That boy was like a saint." "I'd trust that kid with anything I have."[2]

But people like Billy are prime candidates for a shadow side going out of control. Mind you, all of us have that capability, but those who think they have obliterated their shadows and are only what they believe they are and what they appear to be are the most vulnerable. Perhaps that's why Jesus said it is dangerous when all persons speak well of you—because of our tendency to believe every compliment paid us.

It is important for us to remember that when something explodes in us, it was there all the time waiting for some circumstance to light the fuse. One day the sleeping dogs will wake up and terrorize their master and the whole neighborhood. It is far better to come to terms with our shadow before it comes crashing through the basement door with destructive consequences.

Are we left in despair, or is there something we can do? The only safe answer, I believe, is the fourth option—embrace your shadow.

Does that seem like an outrageous option? Hug that dark, mysterious, frightening swamp creature that we've kept under lock and key all these years?

But until we can accept—yes, even "own"—the shadowy side of ourselves, we are not complete persons. We need to incorporate into our conscious self that dark side of our being that is as much a part of us as the brighter, public side we are pleased to show the world.

Only in this way do we achieve wholeness. Owning our sinfulness is the only way we can stand in the grace of God. Otherwise, we think we're so good that we do not need grace. Have a conversation with your shadow along these lines: "Yes, I know you are there, and I acknowledge that you are part of me. I cannot destroy you, but I will not reject you. I am aware of and respect the measure of your power, but I will not allow you to control me. And remember, shadow, that light is more powerful than darkness."

Actually, we need the shadow in order to be whole people, real people. Only things with substance cast shadows. If we had no shadow, we would be unreal, unnatural. Legend has it that only the devil casts no shadow, and that is because he is all evil. Your shadow indentifies you as a whole, solid person.

Moreover, accepting our shadow as a part of us deflates our phony image of perfection. And since we know that we are a mixture of darkness and light, we can relax and quit pretending. Sure, I am a decent person, but I am perfectly capable of being a skunk. I am honest, yet I can be a crook. I am faithful to my wife, but I can also lust. I may be able to lead a nation, but I can also be small and vengeful.

A senior advisor to former President Jimmy Carter, Hedley Donovan, spoke of the "surface paradoxes" evident in that deeply religious man. Among them, Donovan said, was "the man of decency and compassion, with a deeply genuine goodness toward humanity in general, toward many groups, classes and particular individuals, yet also capable of petty and vindictive behavior. He had a long memory and a tendency to impute unworthy motives to those who crossed him. The 'mean streak' was real."[3]

Oh yes, presidents have shadow sides. Preachers have them. And writers, too.

I am the faithful son who stays home and works my father's farm, but I am also the prodigal who spends his inheritance in riotous living. If those brothers in Jesus' story had not been estranged, each could have enhanced the other. The older-brother side could have brought responsibility, thoughtfulness, and maturity to the younger, while the younger-brother side could have added joy, humility, and spontaneity to the older brother.

The acceptance of each other would have brought the brothers not only reconciliation, but integration. The apostle Paul answers his own plea for deliverance when he says that Jesus is the solution to our conflicting character traits. Only Jesus can integrate life's contradictory and opposite sides into one perfect whole—"all things are held together in him" (Col. 1:17).

By the Cross, God has broken the power of evil within us. But when Jesus taught us to pray". . . deliver us from evil," he knew we would always have to struggle with our shadow. By squarely facing our dark side, we are released from its control, but deliverance comes only through the power of the liberating and integrating Christ who brings together both our natures and helps us stop the search for flaws in others.

That's good news for Kingdom people, because it's hard to dance if you're examining everybody else on the floor for specks of sawdust while looking through your own redwood forest.

9. Making Peace with Your Shadow

At first glance, the Sermon on the Mount looks simple. Some parts of it, in fact, seem downright innocuous and trivial. Take this statement by Jesus, for instance, as paraphrased in the Living Bible, "Come to terms quickly with your enemy before it is too late and he drags you into court and you are thrown into a debtor's cell, for you will stay there until you have paid the last penny" (Matt. 5:25–26, LB).

On a casual reading, it sounds like Jesus is simply recommending that lawsuits be settled out of court. That is undoubtedly good advice most of the time, but we would not—nor, I think, would Jesus—necessarily affirm it as good practice in every circumstance in today's complex society. Some cases require a legal judgment and should be allowed to go the full distance. Moreover, in this teaching Jesus indicates we are bound to lose if we go before a judge in a civil suit, when, in fact, the verdict might favor us. Then it would be our opponent who would suffer the consequences.

What then can this teaching mean, and what are its implications for our journey on the strait and narrow? Could making peace with our enemy have something to do with resolving an inner conflict between the two sides of our nature? Is there an adversarial relationship between the dark and light halves of one whole personality, between our shadow side and our persona? Might Jesus be talking about signing a peace treaty to end this civil war that goes on inside us?

One of the early church fathers, Augustine, believed so. In one of his sermons, he wrote, "The Word of God is . . . our adversary as long as we are our own adversaries. As long as thou art thine own enemy, thou hast the Word of God thine enemy; be thine own friend, and thou art in agreement with it."

Some of us may occasionally be aware of an inner conflict, but few of us have given much serious thought to an adversary we carry within ourselves. However, as we saw in the previous chapter, the apostle Paul understood very well the duality of human nature. We are familiar with his plaintive confession: "I don't do the good I want to do; instead, I do the evil I do not want to do. . . . So I find that this law is at work: when I want to do good, what is evil is the only choice I have" (Rom. 7:19, 21, TEV).

It is important to remember that what Jung called the shadow side is not evil *per se*. We may allow it to push us into sinful behavior, but essentially it is our seamy side, which sometimes thinks and acts in ways that are not socially acceptable, causing us to feel shame and embarrassment. For that reason, we try to keep it hidden while displaying for public view our persona, or what we think is the more attractive side of our personality. We do this because we believe people will not like that part of us about which we feel ambivalent.

This means that we make our shadow side an inner adversary to be fought against and suppressed. Jesus acknowledged this dichotomy of personality in human nature, but he stated strongly that denial and suppression are neither healthy nor effective ways of dealing with it. For spiritual wholeness, Jesus said, we must own both the shadow and the light sides as ours and attempt to reconcile the two within us. Otherwise, we are not complete persons.

Such an exercise in peacemaking is difficult, I have discovered, since it means facing an adversary I don't like. But I have found out also that I will pay a heavy price in emotional and spiritual sickness if I fail to do it. I believe this is at least one of the meanings Jesus had in mind when he said, "Every kingdom divided against itself will be ruined" (Matt. 12:25, NIV).

The key to spiritual wholeness and emotional health is integration of the spirit, not division or fragmentation. As John Sanford puts it, "The kingdom of God requires that that the outer man and inner man correspond to each other."[1]

How can we bring these two opposites into harmony? We can do it by transparency and honesty. The more we can accept both the good and the bad of our true selves, the less we need to pretend to be something we aren't. This does not mean surrendering to our shadow's power. That would be a spiritual disaster. But it does mean accepting this so-called enemy as a legitimate part of ourselves so it may be transformed into a creative and useful part of our personality.

Or to put it another way, it means kissing the frog so he may become a prince. Do you remember the fable? Good looking but vain and mean, the prince showed few character traits that befit his noble birth. A witch turned him into a frog, giving him a physical appearance to match his personality. The curse could be lifted only when the frog was kissed by a princess who would love and accept the creature as he really was.

As with so many childhood fairy stories, there is a psychological and spiritual lesson in this one. It is illustrative of a story in the Old Testament (Genesis 25–35) about a man who through great struggle made peace with his shadow. It could be my story—or yours. However, it happens to be that of a Hebrew patriarch named Jacob.

Jacob was his name before the frog became a prince and was given another name. It was less than a princely name, but it was right on target because it revealed the shadow side of his character.

Let's go back to the beginning.

Jacob came from godly stock. His grandfather was Abraham, whose name is listed in faith's Hall of Fame as an obedient pilgrim who became the father of the Hebrew people. Jacob's father was Isaac, the son of Abraham's and Sarah's old age and the miracle child of promise whom his father almost sacrificed to God as an act of unquestioning obedience.

When Isaac became a man, the best thing he ever did was to marry Rebekah. He seems to have been pretty ordinary. She was beautiful, vivacious, gifted, creative, and strong. But a sadness filled her life. She grieved because she could not have children, and this was the only way a woman could fulfill herself in those days. Finally, after twenty years of disappointment, she conceived, but it was a difficult pregnancy. There was continuous struggle in her womb, and since there was no doctor in the neighborhood, Rebekah consulted God.

Here is what God revealed to her:

> "Two nations are in your womb,
> And two peoples from within you will be separated;
> One people will be stronger than the other,
> and the older will serve the younger."
>
> Gen. 25:23, NIV

Rebekah would have twins, and the struggle she felt in her womb was a rivalry between the two that would continue throughout their lives. It started at the moment of their birth. The first one came, and "his skin was like a hairy robe," so he was named Esau, which sounds like the Hebrew word for hair.

Right behind him was the second son with his hand on the heel of the first as if tripping him up. Maybe he knew even then that when you are number two, you have to try harder. It was a prophetic omen, and he was given a name to match—Jacob, the Grabber! It could also be translated "trickster" or "supplanter." So here is our frog with a name that betrayed him wherever he went. "Watch out, here comes the trickster!" the other children would shout. Later it was, "Watch your wallet, the grabber just walked up."

Talk about a shadow side! It is bad enough to have one without also having a name that advertises it like a billboard.

The brothers were total opposites. Esau was impetuous, an outdoorsman, a member of the National Rifle Association, a meat-and-potatoes kind of guy, his father's favorite. Jacob was a mama's boy, contemplative and scholarly, a smooth body with a slick personality to match, an introvert who stayed in his mother's tent much of the time.

All this set the stage for a fascinating drama. It was an ancient custom that the oldest son should receive the father's blessing and birthright to become head of the clan. However, remembering the prophecy spoken privately to her about the older serving the younger, Rebekah set about to overturn this tradition and get the birthright for Jacob.

Rebekah's talent for scheming and manipulation is about to assert itself, revealing her own shadow side.

One day she overheard Isaac tell Esau to go hunting and make some of his favorite venison stew as a prelude to receiving his father's blessing. Rebekah had no time to lose, and her creative mind devised a plan. She made a tasty meat dish for her blind husband and dressed Jacob in Esau's clothes. To enhance the deception she had Jacob put goat hair on his hands and arms so he would feel like Esau. Then she sent Jacob in to his father with the specially prepared imitation venison stew.

Even though afraid he'd be found out, Jacob followed his mother's instructions, hoping Isaac would be tricked into bestowing the patriarchal blessing on him. The old, sightless man was skeptical because of the sound of Jacob's voice, but he felt the goat hair that had been patched in place and smelled the outdoors on Esau's clothes. The deception was complete. Jacob passed the touch-and-smell test with flying colors, thanks to Rebekah's makeup artistry. And with confidence Isaac bestowed his fatherly blessing (Gen. 27:28–29).

As if on cue, just a few minutes after Jacob left his father's tent, Esau arrived with his own stew. A heart-rending scene between father and eldest son followed, but in line with the custom the blessing cannot be revoked. The trickster had done it again!

Esau was furious and vowed revenge, including a terminal solution to the "Jacob problem." Again, Rebekah put her mind to work. On the partially true pretext that she does not want Jacob to marry a pagan Canaanite girl, she persuades Isaac to send Jacob to her brother, Laban, in northern Mesopotamia.

So thanks again to his mother's ingenuity, Jacob is able to counter Esau's "terminal solution," (Jacob's death), with his own "spatial solution," that is, simply putting as much space as he can as fast as he can between himself and his angry brother.

Jacob left home in fear. But the problem with running away is that you can't leave your shadow behind. Jacob takes only his walking stick, his name, and his shadow with him, but the last two make up quite a load of baggage. Nonetheless, it is the start of his spiritual pilgrimage, a journey that will end with the frog becoming a prince.

There is a central truth in this part of the story that is worth highlighting. It is this: God uses "frogs" even before they become "princes." Jacob's experience should encourage us all. God didn't reject Jacob because he had not achieved moral perfection. Rather, he sovereignly incorporated Jacob's shadow side into the divine plan, all the while nudging the trickster toward spiritual insight and maturity.

Often we set standards of perfection for ourselves and others that are so unrealistic that God himself ignores them. How much more honest it is to say simply, "Be patient; God isn't through with me yet."

Every character in this story has a shadow side. The Bible does not cover up their humanity. The portraits are not retouched to eliminate the flaws. Jacob is ruthless, Rebekah is scheming, Esau is impetuous, and Isaac is spiritually insensitive. Yet they all were instruments of God to move forward his plan in human history.

But Jacob still had to face himself and come to terms with his shadow. Only when the frog admitted he was a frog could he believe that it might be possible for him to become a prince. Self-recognition and acknowledgment are the first crucial steps toward making and finding peace.

Throughout the Sermon on the Mount, Jesus holds a mirror in front of us that reflects the true image of our heart, and he says, "That's you." Then we have two choices: we can accept the truth of what he says and be liberated in the disclosure, or we can turn our backs on the truth the way the Pharisees did.

Absolutely nothing aroused the hatred of the Pharisees more than when Jesus held up the mirror of truth that stripped away their pretense. They seethed, they fumed, they ripped their robes; and they crucified the One who showed them the mirror.

Rejecting the truth about themselves, they hardened into evil incarnate, or as Scott Peck puts it in the title of his insightful book on evil, they became "people of the lie."

When Jacob left the security of home and started his journey toward the Kingdom, he was going to get a chance to face himself and see his mirror image. On his first night out, he slept in an open field and had a dream in which he saw God. In his dream he saw a ladder stretching from earth to heaven. God was standing at the top, and angels were moving up and down the ladder.

The Lord spoke to Jacob in the dream and promised that he would inherit the legacy God had promised to Abraham and Isaac. Furthermore, God promised to protect Jacob in his travels and bring him back safely to his homeland (Gen. 28:13–15).

The dream had a profound effect on Jacob. It was, after all, his first personal encounter with God. Up to this point, Jacob had relegated God to a historical and family status; Yahweh was his father's God and the God of his clan. On a daily basis, however, Jacob had been his own god.

Jacob was awestruck by his vision of the living God and fumbled around trying to decide how to act. He attempted to strike a materialistic deal with God, promising to serve God if God would take care of him. As childish as his concept of God was— somewhere between Santa Claus and a heavenly piñata—it does represent some spiritual progress.

This first step outside himself would ultimately clear up his confusion about which one is God and which one is the frog. It seems that up to this point in his life, Jacob had not given much thought to this distinction.

His second insight into his own character came when he finally stumbled out of the wilderness into his Uncle Laban's tent. In this relationship, Jacob meets his match. Laban is Jacob's mirror image, only more experienced, and the younger con artist doesn't like what he sees in that dark mirror.

The pace of the story picks up as Jacob falls in love with Laban's daughter, the beautiful Rachel, and agrees to a seven-year work contract if he can marry her. When the contract was fulfilled, however, Laban switched his oldest daughter, Leah, into the marriage tent and bed. With one clever stroke Laban outfoxed the fox—Jacob the deceiver was himself deceived.

Listen to Jacob's outrage the next morning, "Why did you do this to me? I worked seven years for Rachel. Why have you tricked me?" (see Gen. 29:25).

What an amazing question from the trickster! Oh, the irony. How puritanical we can be—preachers and televangelists not excluded—when we meet our own shadow in someone else.

Laban has a perfectly logical answer. The only problem is that apparently it took him seven years to remember it. Why, he says in mock amazement, he doesn't know how it is back where Jacob came from, but the custom of his society forbade him to marry off his younger daughter ahead of the older one. Then Laban has a ready solution to the problem—Jacob can sign another seven-year work contract for Rachel.

Jacob agreed. And every day he worked for Laban he was forced to look into the mirror of Laban's face. Finally, armed with this insight, Jacob left with his family and his cattle, ready for the climactic struggle that would end in his making peace with his shadow.

There's a central truth in this part of the story as well. It is this: the path toward self-discovery most often begins in a wilderness experience. We must be forced out of security and comfort before we will undertake the unpleasant task of facing that part of ourselves we have suppressed or denied.

For some of us, the lonely and frightening wilderness journey may begin with a death, a serious illness, a divorce, an economic setback, a career change, a relocation, or some other disruption of the status quo.

It is possible that some people who find a higher motivation for spiritual growth may never need to go through a wilderness experience. Others are able to learn the lessons of the wilderness quickly and don't need to spend much time there. However, some of us, like Moses, who required forty years in the desert, find that self-awareness and growth come slowly and with pain.

But there is something positive about a wilderness experience. It gives us an opportunity to have a new beginning. Such being the case, treat it as a friend; follow where the path takes you. If we don't struggle against the wilderness experience, we will find in it a gentle teacher of Kingdom truths.

The theologian Walter Brueggemann observed one time, "Deep in our history is this incredible story that says wilderness is a place of nourishment, that precariousness is a way of life, that vulnerability is a source of wholeness. Because God meets us in the wilderness, God accepts the wilderness as the place for being God and our place for being his people." What makes it redemptive is the awareness that we are on our way to becoming a prince or princess.

Jacob's final, life-changing encounter occurred on his way back home. All his life Jacob had been an escapist. His way of coping was to run away—from his brother, from himself, from unpleasant circumstances. So it was necessary for God to send him back home to face up to Esau and to his own shadow. He must be reconciled to his brother and himself.

The story now rushes toward a climax. Esau got word of Jacob's coming. Next, Jacob sent a negotiating team on ahead, but they returned with the disturbing news that Esau was on the road with an army of four hundred men. Jacob was frantic, but this time he didn't run away—he didn't try the spatial solution. Instead he relied on a strategem. He divided his household into two groups, hoping to save half his possessions from Esau's vengeance. Then he sent a peace offering—350 head of cattle—to his brother.

And, finally, in his extremity, Jacob prayed. It was a touching and honest prayer. He admitted he was unworthy. He reflected on the fact that he had left home with only a walking stick and that God had made him a wealthy man with a clan of his own. Then he confessed that he was scared. And he reminded God of the early promise of safety and deliverance.

In an unselfish act that indicates some inner change had already taken place, instead of hiding behind his family, Jacob moved them out of harm's way across the Jabbok River. And with rare spiritual courage, he sat down alone to wait for his brother.

That night the Bible says that a mysterious Presence came and wrestled with Jacob. As he struggled with this divine Adversary we can only guess at some of the questions that went racing through Jacob's mind. Who was it? Jacob was sure it was a numinous expression of God. But why? Was he going to die estranged from Esau? Would the frog never make it to princehood?

But there are even deeper questions. Was this wrestling match symbolic of his lifelong inner struggle? Was he finally facing and coming to terms with his dark side? There seems to be no question about it. Whatever else the all-night struggle signified, it was Jacob's chance to make peace with his shadow. As day began to dawn, the Adversary still hadn't defeated Jacob, so he touched Jacob's thigh, and it immediately went out of joint. The fight also went out of the crippled Jacob, but he still held on.

"I won't let you go until you bless me," he told the Man. But there was some unfinished business to be dealt with before the blessing could come. It was in the form of a strange question: "What is your name?" the Presence asks, as if He didn't already know. It was another way of saying, "Acknowledge yourself. Quit trying to run away from your shadow. Be who you are. Own up to your name."

The answer was virtually spat out: "Jacob!" It was more than a name. It was his autobiography.

I have to believe that the eyes of the strugglers met for a long moment. The tension was broken. The frog admits he is a frog! Jacob has made peace with his shadow. He releases his adversary. The conflict is over. Jacob is free.

The sun comes up over a new world for the trickster. And then the miracle happens! "Your name is no longer Jacob," the Presence tells him. "It is Israel, a prince of God." His new name suggests royalty and power. The frog has been kissed. And although the prince would be lame in the hip for the rest of his life, his limp was a humbling reminder of what he once had been.

Suddenly, all the rest of life began to fall into place. The reconciliation with Esau is tearful and total. God prospers Jacob as he had promised. And the patriarch goes down to his grave surrounded by his children and grandchildren, an old man at peace with God, with the world and with himself.

What spiritual insight is to be gained here? Simply this: The truth shall make you free. What an expansive principle! When the frog acknowledged the truth of his character, he was liberated from the fear of having his secret discovered. It was no longer a secret. He was free from having to pretend. And having been made a new person, he was free to grow and change.

It has never been summed up more simply and beautifully than in this testimony by an old southern granny, "I know I ain't what I oughta be, and I know I ain't what I'm gonna be, but, thank God, I ain't what I was."

That is the joyous witness of every frog who has been transformed into a prince by the kiss of acceptance. And princes never lack for somebody to take to the dance.

10. The Treasures of the Kingdom

His name was James. But right up to the time he died at eighty-five, we all called him Jimmy—affectionately, of course, and probably because of his diminutive size. It certainly was no disrespect to his talent, which was big. I'm talking about Jimmy Cagney, the actor.

Mr. Cagney once gave this advice to a desperate newcomer in his profession, "Walk in, plant yourself, look the other fellow in the eye and tell the truth."

When Jesus stepped out of the wings of eternity onto the stage of human history, that is exactly what he did. In his day, that was a radical way to introduce yourself. Then, as now, compliance and unquestioning acceptance of the system was the way to gain prestige and honors. Conformity would get you peer approval, a testimonial banquet and Rabbi Emeritus at sixty-five, plus several honorary degrees on your way to retirement.

Jesus walked in, planted his feet, looked the world in the eye and told the truth. He got a cross at thirty-three.

The British writer Dorothy Sayers described him this way, "The people who hanged Christ never accused him of being a bore—on the contrary, they thought him too dynamic to be safe. . . . It has been left to later generations to muffle up that shattering personality and surround him with the atmosphere of tedium. We have very efficiently pared the claws of the Lion of Judah, certified him 'meek and mild,' and recommended him as a fitting household pet for pale curates and pious old ladies.

"To those who knew him, however, he in no way suggested a milk-and-water person; they objected to him as a dangerous firebrand. True, he was tender to the unfortunate, patient with honest inquirers and humble before heaven; but he insulted respectable clergymen by calling them hypocrites; he referred to King Herod as 'that fox'; He went to parties in disreputable company and was looked upon as a 'gluttonous man and a winebibber, a friend of publicans and sinners'; He insulted indignant tradesmen and threw them and their belongings out of the temple; . . . He showed no proper deference for wealth or social position; . . . But He had 'a daily beauty in his life that made us ugly,' and officialdom felt that the established order of things would be more secure without him.

"So," she says, "they did away with God in the name of peace and quietness."[1]

Never was Jesus more radical than when he planted his feet, looked us in the eye, and told us the truth about material possessions and worldly concerns. In his value system, Kingdom interests got first priority.

Jesus knows that our priorities are all topsy-turvy. He is aware how closely our sense of well-being and security is tied up with material things. And because he knows our nature so well and sees us fret and fume over life's ordinary needs, he admonishes us against grasping for those things, "Do not be anxious, saying, 'What shall we eat?' or 'What shall we drink?' or 'What shall we wear?' For the Gentiles seek all these things, and your heavenly Father knows that you need them all" (Matt. 6:31-32).

Those are the overriding concerns of the world; they do not reflect Kingdom values. Jesus wants us to be free from anxiety and worry. To relieve our apprehension about our daily needs, Jesus tries to improve our understanding of God. The provision of these daily necessities has nothing to do with us, he says, but it has everything to do with our heavenly Father.

Listen to how cogently Jesus reasons, "Look at the birds of the air, that they do not sow, neither do they reap, nor gather into barns, and yet your heavenly Father feeds them. Are you not worth much more than they? And which of you by being anxious can add a single cubit to his life's span.

"And why are you anxious about clothing? Observe how the lilies of the field grow; they do not toil nor do they spin, yet I say to you that even Solomon in all his glory did not clothe himself like one of these" (Matt. 6:26-29, NASB).

Jesus then makes this radical and improbable statement, suggesting that all these earthly things are the direct benefit of living by the principles of the Kingdom, "But seek first his kingdom and his righteousness and all these things shall be yours as well" (Matt. 6:33).

This is Jesus' radical concept: the treasures come with the Kingdom. They are not extraneous to it or separated from it. They are what business calls the perquisites—the unearned benefits—that go with working for the company. They are in the contract for Kingdom people. You may be thinking, "That all sounds so good. I'd sure like to be free from the tyranny of material anxieties, but I don't understand this Kingdom business. What is it? Where is it? What's the relationship between a spiritual kingdom and material things? I like Jesus' promise, but I am troubled by the conditions."

In response to these questions, let's first try to find out something about the Kingdom of God. It is the hinge phrase on which so many of Jesus' teachings swing. You will find it in Mark's Gospel thirteen times. It is used in Luke's Gospel twenty-eight times and thirty-eight times in the Gospel of Matthew. In fact, Matthew's Gospel has been called "the Gospel of the Kingdom" because in it Jesus introduces twelve of his parables with the expression, "The kingdom of heaven is like . . ."

Jesus then goes on to say that the Kingdom of heaven is close at hand, that we have to be born from above in order to see it, that we can't get into it unless we become like a little child, that we can't find it unless our goodness is deeper than that of the Pharisees. Then he shocks his listeners by saying that tax collectors and prostitutes will get into the Kingdom ahead of self-righteous religious leaders, and that the Kingdom is of such singular value as to be like a pearl of great price, worth selling everything else we own to possess.

Finally, Jesus says, the Kingdom is not external but within us.

There are so many of Jesus' teachings that sound like mystery and paradox. In fact, he spoke of the Kingdom only in picture language and metaphor. When the disciples asked why he used so many parables in teaching, Jesus said, "To you it has been given to know of the kingdom of heaven, but to them it has not been given" (Matt. 13:11). That was not arbitrary discriminaton, however. He invited anyone to hear who has ears to hear, indicating that those who were teachable could understand the truths about the Kingdom. Surely this is part of the truth into which he promised the Holy Spirit will guide us.

Perhaps our problem in understanding is that we have tried to be too profound in looking for the Kingdom. We seem to have forgotten that Jesus wasn't giving a road map to theologians. Rather, he was speaking to illiterate peasants who didn't even know how to spell seminary, much less ever hope to attend one. As my wife, Nancy, said to me one day, "You may be too smart to find the Kingdom, but you can't be too dumb."

Whatever mysteries are connected with the Kingdom, there are some things we clearly know. Let's concentrate on those.

First, we know where the Kingdom is and where it is not. It is not tangible or material. It is not defined in political, economic, or military terms. If we seek it in the physical realm, we'll be looking in the wrong place. When Jesus said that "the Kingdom of God is within you" (Luke 17:21, TEV), he was telling us that it is a very personal reality, not a system or an institution.

The Kingdom is here among us, we discover it individually through the process of inner change. One of the reasons it is good news is that it is within the reach of any of us. Another reason it is good news is that the Kingdom is very much a here-and-now experience. Don't try to push it off as some future event coming on us from the outside. True, Jesus taught us to pray, "Thy kingdom come," but it is in the future only because it is working itself out. It is also in the present, like a baby in the womb. A fetus has all the essential parts of a body, but they are not yet fully developed.

So it is with the embryonic Kingdom within us. Jesus said it starts out as a tiny seed and grows to be the largest of trees. Several times he emphasized that the Kingdom of heaven is close at hand. So the Kingdom is not outside us, but within us; it is not experienced in some physical sense, but in spiritual rebirth; it can happen now, not just later; it is personal, not institutional.

But how can we recognize it when we experience it, and what is it like? Something that happened to me in 1966 speaks to these kinds of questions and illuminates the point I want to make.

My mission was to go to Ethiopia to invite His Imperial Majesty, Emperor Haile Selassie, to address an international conference sponsored by Billy Graham. I was an American living in Berlin, Germany, at the time, but as soon as I boarded the plane, I knew I was under the influence of the Ethiopian emperor. The plane bore his symbol, an imperial lion holding a scepter in its paw. When we landed in Addis Ababa, his symbol was everywhere—at the airport, in the hotel, on the taxis, on the street signs. There was no doubt about it, I was in Haile Selassie's kingdom.

When my taxi entered the driveway to the palace, we drove between two live, caged imperial lions, another reminder of who ruled the kingdom. Everything that represented the king, including his pet chihuahua, was revered.

In this whole experience, I saw a parable of the Kingdom of God. The king's domain is everywhere the king's influence is felt, his symbol is displayed, and his name is honored. That's how we can determine where the Kingdom of God is. That's the way we can know whether or not we have the Kingdom within. Do we acknowledge God's authority in our lives? Do we display his symbol—which is love—in our relationships? Do we live in such a way as to honor and hallow his name rather than demean and shame it?

If we can answer yes to those questions, that's what it means to seek God's Kingdom first.

Next comes another question: What else do we know about the Kingdom? We know that it is experienced through repentance. The text for Jesus' first sermon was "Repent, for the kingdom of heaven is at hand." But just what does it mean to repent?

Repent is an action verb. Though it has to do with a change of attitude, there is no true repentance until our attitude has brought a change of direction. We leave the broad road that is going one way and get on the narrow road that runs in the opposite direction. To repent means to turn away from the world's value system and accept the values of God's Kingdom. We can't go east and west at the same time.

Jesus says that pagans can't help but be preoccupied with material things. But Kingdom people should have a different set of priorities. And Jesus makes it clear that we are not to be concerned with stockpiling even the so-called necessities of life. Repentance is when we start to live as if there were concerns in life other than material ones.

When we reach that place, we start to understand that people and institutions are merely channels of God's supply and provision, while God is our only Source. I came into a church vocation at the age of twenty, and for nearly forty years I believed that the church or some other religious organization was the source of my livelihood. Although no one ever said it in so many words and it certainly wasn't in any contract, there was a kind of unspoken agreement that if I looked after the things of God assigned to me, the institutions of religion would look after me.

Then, at age fifty-seven, I found myself outside this unwritten agreement. I had no job and received no calls or invitations to speak. I thought of a few people I knew who might provide employment. In desperation, I started looking to them as a primary source because I knew of no others.

When no one responded, I panicked. I had never before been without a place to go. What would I do to earn a living?

Oral Roberts had a word for me in that critical time. He said, "Stan, you've been looking to the wrong place. God is the Source. He has the overflowing and inexhaustible supply. He uses all kinds of people and organizations to deliver the supply, but they are only channels. Start looking to the primary Source, and God may surprise you in his selection of a channel."

So Nancy and and I started focusing our thoughts on God and trusting him as our Source. I no longer felt that those others had let me down. It wasn't their fault. They had no way of knowing just how much I needed them.

Oral was right. God surprised us—and keeps on surprising us—with the channels he uses to deliver his supply to meet our needs. And we keep on trying to learn the lessons of simple faith and total trust.

Because this attitude and behavior is so radically different from that practiced by the world, John Sanford strikes me as being right when he says, "The entrance to the kingdom is often a violent one, for entering into the kingdom means surrendering the old personality and finding a new wine."[2] Jesus says this new wine requires new wineskins, or a new person, so it is in keeping with his picture language to refer to the experience as being "born again." What happens when you pass through this crisis into the fullness of the Kingdom is so radical that to describe it requires that kind of dramatic language.

There is at least one other thing we should say about the Kingdom—another condition for entering it. Jesus said, "I assure you that unless you change and become like children you will never enter the Kingdom of heaven" (Matt. 18:3, TEV). Don't be scared of this experience. God is not recruiting for an overpopulated nursery school. He doesn't mean for us to regress and become childish. In fact, he means the very opposite. To become like children means for our adult selves to discover the child self within us—that part of us from which springs spontaneity, imagination, and freshness.

We work so hard at making the Christian life sophisticated, dull, and boring. The Pharisees had succeeded in making the Kingdom a rational, adult experience, so that one of their big criticisms of Jesus was that he not only went to parties, he actually enjoyed them!

In 1986, a treasure-hunting crew led by Mel Fisher found the ruins of the Spanish galleon *Atocha* off the Florida Keys after searching for it for sixteen years. It was loaded with treasure valued at more than $400 million. When divers brought up the first tokens of this bounty, they hugged each other, broke out the champagne, and danced on the deck. They acted, well, just like kids! And why not? They had found the treasure.

Jesus said the coming of the Kingdom is like a wedding, a party, a feast. And who knows better how to celebrate occasions like that than a child, or one who still has a free and unstructured connection to the inner world? When I take off the mask, tear down the false facade, act and speak honestly, and express what I feel without hypocrisy—in other words, when I become as a little child—I am seeking first the Kingdom.

And those who find the Kingdom also find the treasure.

We've spent so much time exploring Jesus' teachings about the Kingdom because that's where the treasure is. Find the Kingdom and you get the benefits, not as a door prize, but because they go with the territory. They are a part of his promise, "Seek ye first the kingdom of God and his righteousness, and all these things shall be added unto you" (Matt. 6:33, KJV).

What things? All we need of everything we need. Guaranteed. It's as good as money in the bank—better, in fact, considering the failure rate of banks today. God's bank is failproof, and when we become a Kingdom person, he opens an account in our name. It isn't just a maintenance account; it is an inheritance account. It's there to meet all our needs. Paul tells the Christians at Philippi, "My God will supply every need of yours according to his riches in glory in Christ Jesus" (Phil. 4:19).

Unfortunately, though, most of the Kingdom accounts are sitting there inactive because we've never drawn on them.

When we have needs, we should try a little exercise. Face them straight out, and tell God about them. Don't be general; be specific. Name them, and list them. Don't avoid them because they seem too terrifying. That will only prolong the anxiety.

Then visualize God as the Source of supply. It is God who will supply every need, and the channels he uses may well surprise you. Meditate on these marvelous words, "Trust in the Lord and do good . . . delight yourself in the Lord and he will give you the desires of your heart" (Ps. 37:3-4).

If you are a Kingdom person, he gives you the desire so that you may desire it.

As the final step in this exercise, get ready to receive God's provision. And don't tell God how he ought to do it. He loves to surprise us. He delights in hearing us say, "Aha!" because that means we recognize that we didn't do it ourselves. We can rationalize away what I call the "surprise factor" of the Kingdom, but we'll miss a lot of fun if we do.

Always remember that the overflowing supply is in the Kingdom. Looking outside the Kingdom will bring only disappointment and failure. In the late nineteenth century, Russell Conwell wrote a very famous book called *Acres of Diamonds* in which he told the legend of Golconda, the most famous gem mine in the world.

A man named Ali Hafed who lived on the banks of the Indus River left his lovely home and family to search for diamonds. He was already a rich man, but he wanted more—he wanted to buy empires and thrones for his children.

Ali Hafed sold his farm at a distressed price, left his family with a neighbor, and set out on his search. Years went by, and he was reduced to rank poverty. A broken man, he threw himself into the sea and was drowned.

Later, the man who bought Ali Hafed's farm took his camel to the river to drink. In the white sand, he saw something sparkling and stooped to pick up a stone. It was a diamond, the first of a trove of gems mined at Golconda. The legendary mine turned out to be right in the middle of Ali Hafed's farm.

The Persian storyteller said to Dr. Conwell, "Had Ali Hafed remained at home—had he dug in his own garden, or in his own fields—instead of poverty, starvation, and death in a strange land, he would have had acres of diamonds."

The story ends with Dr. Conwell saying, "Alas! So many wander away, and fail of finding anything of value."

That story might well have been one of Jesus' parables, for that's how he would have described the relationship of the treasure to the Kingdom. If we've got the Kingdom, if we are in the domain of the King, we've got it all.

It is like buying a piece of land in *fee simple*. It is not a lease, nor is it simply a license to use. It means you have absolute ownership with unrestricted rights. Fee simple is the most commonly used and widely recognized type of real estate ownership. As a legal term it means "ownership of title to real property without limitation or end; in perpetuity." When God gives us the Kingdom in *fee simple*, he doesn't hold back any of the territorial rights, and he doesn't renege on his promise.

We have the same words in the Gospel of Luke about seeking the Kingdom, but here the writer adds a further word from Jesus, "Fear not, little flock, for it is your Father's good pleasure to give you the the kingdom" (Luke 12:32).

Arnold Palmer, the professional golfer, once played a series of exhibition matches in Saudi Arabia. The king was very pleased and proposed to make Arnie a gift. Palmer tried to decline, saying, "You don't have to do that, Your Highness. It is an honor just to be invited to promote golf in your country."

But the king was insistent, "It would offend the custom of my country if you would not receive a gift from me."

After a moment's thought, Arnie said, "Then how about giving me a golf club? That would be a beautiful memento of my visit here."

The next day, delivered to the hotel where Palmer was staying was the title to a golf club on hundreds of acres, with trees, lakes, and a clubhouse!

After telling this story, Brennan Manning adds, "In the presence of a King, don't ask for small gifts."[3]

We are pilgrims on the strait and narrow, and God delights in giving us the Kingdom . . . and all the treasure that is to be found in it.

The point of this part of the Sermon on the Mount is to help us see the futility of worry. Jesus says there are two days about which nobody should ever worry—yesterday and tomorrow. If we must fret about something, he advises, let it be about today, although we should know that God has that under control, as well.

Most of us have been in a J. C. Penney store at some time in our lives, but you may not know that Mr. Penney was a Christian who built his business empire on the Golden Rule. In the crash of 1929, his business was solid, but he had made some unwise personal investments. Consequently, he became so worried that he couldn't sleep. Then he developed shingles, a disorder of the nerves that is both annoying and painful. He was hospitalized and given sedatives but didn't get any relief.

A combination of circumstances had broken him so completely, physically and mentally, that he was overwhelmed with a fear of death. That first night in the hospital he wrote farewell letters to his wife and son because he didn't expect to live till morning.

The next morning he heard singing in the hospital chapel. He pulled himself together and walked down the hall to the chapel where the people were singing "God Will Take Care of You." When they finished, someone read a Scripture lesson and offered a prayer.

Mr. Penney later described what happened: "I can't explain it. I can only call it a miracle. I felt as if I had been instantly lifted out of the darkness of a dungeon into warm, brilliant sunlight. I felt as if I had been transported from hell to paradise. I felt the power of God as I have never felt it before. I knew that God with his love was there to help me. From that day till this, my life has been free from worry.

"I am seventy-one years old, and the most dramatic and glorious minutes of my life were those I spent in that chapel that morning: *God Will Take Care of You.*"[4]

To live free from the anxiety and tyranny of material things, we must find the liberty and joy of Kingdom living. We can trust God, the Source, for all our needs. And as we put Kingdom values first, we'll be surprised at the unknown channels God will use to provide our daily needs.

Welcome to the party, and join all of those who have found the freedom to dance on the strait and narrow. We are celebrating the discovery of the treasures of the Kingdom. And as part of the litany of celebration, we raise our voices using a prayer of Dag Hammarskjöld, "For all that has been, thanks! For all that shall be, yes!"

Notes

PREFACE

1. Fynn, *Mister God, This Is Anna* (New York: Ballantine Books, 1976), p. 78.

INTRODUCTION

1. Robert Farrar Capon, *The Parables of the Kingdom* (Grand Rapids: Zondervan, 1985), p. 58.
2. Brennan Manning, *The Wisdom of Accepted Tenderness* (Danville, NJ: Dimension Books, 1978), p. 34.
3. John A. Sanford, *The Kingdom Within* (Ramsey, NJ: Paulist Press, 1970), p. 19.

CHAPTER 1

1. Ben Campbell Johnson, *Matthew and Mark, a Relational Paraphrase* (Waco, TX: Word Books, 1978), p. 29.
2. Ibid., p. 22.
3. R. G. B. Tasker, *The Gospel According to St. Matthew*, Tyndale New Testament Commentary Series (Grand Rapids: Eerdmans, 1979), p. 69.
4. Manning, *Wisdom of Accepted Tenderness*, p. 62–63.

CHAPTER 2

1. Herman Wouk, *Inside, Outside* (Boston: Little, Brown, 1985), p. 246–49.
2. Viktor Frankl, *Man's Search for Meaning* (New York: Washington Square Press, 1963), p. 141–42.

CHAPTER 3

1. Edwin Markham, "Outwitted," *Poems of Edwin Markham* (New York: Harper & Brothers, 1950), p. 18.

CHAPTER 4

1. Robert Farrar Capon, *Hunting the Divine Fox* (Minneapolis: Seabury Press, 1974), p. 132.
2. Lewis B. Smedes, *Forgive and Forget* (San Francisco: Harper & Row, 1984), p. 24–25.
3. John Perkins, *Let Justice Roll Down* (Ventura, CA: Regal Books, 1976) p. 154–65.
4. Corrie ten Boom, *The Hiding Place* (Minneapolis: World Wide Publications, 1971), p. 233.

CHAPTER 5

1. Dale Carnegie, *How to Stop Worrying and Start Living* (New York: Simon & Schuster, 1948), p. 101.

CHAPTER 6

1. *Time*, March 3, 1980.

2. Oscar Wilde, *The Picture of Dorian Gray* (New York: Washington Square Press, Pocket Books, 1972), pp. 25–26.
3. Ibid., p. 223.
4. Frankl, *Man's Search for Meaning*, p. 3.
5. Holly Brubach, "Ralph Lauren's Achievement," *Atlantic Monthly*, August 1987.
6. Stan Mooneyham, *Traveling Hopefully* (Waco, TX: Word Books, 1984), p. 15.

CHAPTER 7

1. Johnson, *Matthew and Mark*, p. 24.
2. Dietrich Bonhoeffer, *Life Together* (New York: Harper & Row, 1954), p. 110.
3. C. S. Lewis, *The Great Divorce* (New York: Macmillan, 1946), pp. 33–34.

CHAPTER 8

1. William A. Miller, *Make Friends with Your Shadow* (Minneapolis: Augsburg Publishing House, 1981), p. 71.
2. Ibid., adapted from a story on p. 63–64.
3. Hedley Donovan, *Roosevelt to Reagan: A Reporter's Encounters with Nine Presidents* (New York: Harper & Row, 1985).

CHAPTER 9

1. Sanford, *Kingdom Within*, p. 109.

CHAPTER 10

1. Dorothy Sayers, *The Greatest Drama Ever Staged* (London: Hodder and Stoughton, 1938).
2. Sanford, *Kingdom Within*, p. 79.
3. Brennan Manning, *Lion and Lamb* (Old Tappan, NJ: Chosen Books, 1986), p. 165.
4. Carnegie, *How to Stop Worrying*, pp. 253–54.